THE SEARCH FOR THOMAS MANESS

ELIZABETH A. SAUNDERS

Tannery Books

The Search for Thomas Maness
Copyright ©2024 by Elizabeth A. Saunders

All rights reserved. No portion of this work may be reproduced or used in any manner whatsoever without the permission of the author. For permissions contact the author.

The Search for Thomas Maness
By Elizabeth A. Saunders
1. Biography & Autobiography: Criminals & Outlaws 2. Family & Relationships: Family History & Genealogy
ISBN: 979-8-99179-423-7
Library of Congress Control Number 2024923026

Join the community at elizabethasaunders.com

Book Design by Sarah Katreen Hoggatt, Book Layout Biz
Cover Design by Getcovers

Printed in the United States of America
Tannery Books, 331 Wynnewood Drive, Archdale, N.C. 27263

*Dedicated to
Frank Oscar Maness
who encouraged and helped me
and to all of our extended Maness clan*

CONTENTS

INTRODUCTION - vii
1. Signing Up - 1
2. Inheritance - 5
3. Initiation - 9
4. Starting the Search - 13
5. Crossing - 15
6. Clues and Stories - 19
7. Malvern Hill - 23
8. Deserters - 29
9. Shadrach - 31
10. Alexander - 33
11. Gettysburg - 39
12. Survivor - 43
13. From the Fire into the Frying Pan - 47
14. Ghost Stories - 51
15. Prisoner of War - 55
16. Shadrach - 59
17. Elmira Prison Camp - 63
18. Moving Home - 71
19. Home - 75
20. Back to the Mystery - 79
21. Pandora - 81
22. Nancy - 85
23. Oral History - 87
24. Traveling Man - 91
25. Lacy Garner and Thurman Maness - 95

26   DNA Genealogy · 99
27   Martha · 103
28   Sarah · 105
29   Search for the Living · 107
30   Back to DNA · 115
31   Final Tall Tale · 119

Legacy

Brothers and Sisters and Brothers in Arms · 125
The Maynor Family · 131
Our Maness Clan · 135
The Manes–Sifford Family · 141
The Maners Family · 145
The Manes–Foreman–Walker Family · 149
Martha Mashburn's Unusual Family · 153
The Maness-Jones Family · 155

Epilogue · 157

Acknowledgements · 159

Appendix: Thomas S. Maness' Birth Date · 161

Bibliography · 163

Notes · 171

Index · 197

INTRODUCTION

This book is a work of nonfiction. Facts are cited, and the rich but less reliable oral history has been cited as well. However, I have taken the following liberties to enhance the story.

First, modern conversations are presented in the sense that I remember them, meaning that the exact words have been lost but the sense preserved. Repetitive conversations, meals, and encounters over the years have been meshed into single scenes. Names have been added to conversations where, in real life, a complex system of family nicknames was used, such as "Sis" and "Honey." My grandparents rarely called each other by their given names; Papaw called his wife "Momma" and she called him "Daddy." My uncle not only called his mother "Mother," he also referred to his sisters as "Mother" when talking to their children. Even I got confused! He called his sisters "Sis" to their faces unless there was a subtle argument going on, and then given names were used. I have added the given names—without the arguments—to minimize confusion.

When I transcribed the single tape recording of an interview with Thurman Maness, I realized that as I listened at the time (and in my memory, later), I automatically interpreted our local dialect, corrected grammar, and deleted many repetitive phrases. Since lengthy word-for-word quotes changed the tone of the scene from the way I remember it and since I didn't have recordings of the other interviews, I used the transcription more for fact checking and inserted small excerpts or kept the summarized dialogue. For example, when Thurman mentioned a woman from Randolph County (which is how I remembered it), the actual dialogue was a many-sentence exchange about some folks from near High Point asking about a man with an "S" in his name ... that finally ended in a mention of Randolph County. I have hopefully kept the truth of the encounter and the stories, while condensing more than 8,800 words of dialogue.

The other liberty is to imply Thomas Maness' first-hand experience in everything Company H of the Twenty-Sixth North Carolina regiment experienced, except where muster rolls or other records document his absence. Barring the remote possibility he could have been left with the rear guard during a battle (a group of men assigned to guard the horses and supplies), participation in every battle is the most likely scenario. Thomas left no record that will ever tell us what was going through his mind. Any parts where I have implied his thoughts or feelings came from written memoirs of other men in the regiment or from oral history about Thomas passed down by relatives. Historical comments in quotation have been taken from written contemporary reports and memoirs or from modern oral history interviews.

A word of caution to readers: if you want to read this true story like a novel, avoid turning to the endnotes. Citations may contain spoilers!

CHAPTER 1
SIGNING UP

Carthage, Moore County, North Carolina, June 3, 1861

Thomas must have wondered if he'd get away with it. If Captain William P. Martin gave him a second look, the Confederate Army's need for recruits overruled any doubts he had about the boy's age. Martin filled in the name, "Thomas S. Maness," age eighteen. The dark-haired boy made his mark, drawing a small x.[1] Now a soldier in the army of the Confederate States of America, Thomas was probably pretty pleased with himself. Growing tall ran in the family. He was only around eleven years old.[2]

Thomas had no schooling, no status, nothing to miss at home. Where was home, anyway? Orphaned as children, he and five siblings had been passed around among family members in a region where most heads of household listed themselves as farmers, but the sandy soil produced little but pine trees. Moore County, North Carolina was more about harvesting trees and producing turpentine. These industries profited big landowners and shipbuilders, not poor families and "extra" kids like Thomas. The inability to read or write was not uncommon in rural, nineteenth-century Moore County. Public schools did not exist, so only families with extra money could hire teachers for their sons.

Thomas enlisted at the first opportunity, before his older brothers, Alexander and Shadrach. He wasn't alone, though. He joined up with members of his extensive Maness clan and neighbors from the northwest part of the county, Scottish descendants with names like Campbell, MacDonald, McCaskill and Wallace. Thomas' older relatives, Jonas Sedberry Maness and Bradley Brady, were among the nearly one hundred "Moore County Boys" who signed up those first three days of June 1861.

They converged with men from neighboring counties at Company Shops (the future Burlington) to catch the train to Raleigh. With the railroad less than a decade old, people were touting trains as the eighth wonder of the world. A small village boomed around the centralized maintenance shops for the North Carolina Railroad Company. Thomas saw giant brick buildings large enough to drive engines and cars into from the roundtable. Clanging from the blacksmith shop and the buzzing of wood saws mingled with the chugging of trains and an occasional steam whistle. Smoke drifted through the air from engines still fired by wood.[3]

Thomas and his friends not only got to see these giant, noisy machines, they got to board the cars for the ride to Raleigh. When they reached the capital city, the men disembarked and marched to Camp Crabtree. They set up camp just after dark in an assigned spot near other North Carolina troops. The new recruits started out so green even their officers didn't know what to do. They awoke in the morning to a lively camp with hints of war, including guards at their posts. Corporal John R. Lane and two other men were mysteriously summoned to the commandant, Major Henry K. Burgwyn Jr.

The mystery was solved when the officers returned, humbled by the young major with such command presence. They had failed to take roll call and report in. As punishment, the company was assigned to litter detail. Lane wrote, "This cheering order completely knocked the starch out of our shirts and helped greatly to settle us down to a soldier's life. The cleanliness of the camp was reported by the officer of the day as being perfect. You may be sure our officers reported the company promptly after that."[4]

The Moore County Independents, as they came to be called, became officially designated as Company H of the Twenty-Sixth North

Carolina Troops, Infantry. The men of the Twenty-Sixth Regiment came from counties that had originally opposed secession. Sentiments had changed back in April, when President Lincoln ordered Governor Ellis to supply seventy-five thousand soldiers to attack other southern states. If they had to fight either way, the Carolinians would rather fight the North than against their kinsmen and neighbors.

Capt. Zebulon B. Vance was elected as colonel, but reported for duty later, so nineteen-year-old Lt. Col. Burgwyn (promoted from major), "the boy colonel," was in charge of the regiment. Though young, the handsome and quick-minded Burgwyn, a graduate of the University of North Carolina and Virginia Military Institute, had no problem issuing orders. He awed some and annoyed others, insisting on constant drill and discipline.[5]

Thomas drilled twice a day, from eight to ten o'clock in the morning and again from three to five in the afternoon. He probably enjoyed the initial excitement of army life. He was issued a musket or rifle and drew rations so he could eat every day.[6] Among his counterparts above the Mason-Dixon line, Union soldier Rosetta Wakeman (alias Private Lyons Wakeman) passed as a man to escape a hard life of farming and poverty, similar to the life Thomas had left. Wakeman wrote to her parents, "I [am] enjoying my Self better this summer than I ever did before in this world. I have good Clothing and enough to eat and nothing to do, only to handle my gun and that I can do as well as the rest of them."[7]

On August 29, 1861, a wave of excitement buzzed through Camp Crabtree — Union forces had taken Fort Hatteras on the North Carolina coast. Thomas and his fellow troops packed up supplies and boarded the train in Raleigh on September 2. They travelled all day, as the flat fields of eastern North Carolina flowed by. Thomas arrived in Morehead City at night and slept in the train car. The next day, the regiment marched to Bogue Banks and set up camp.[8]

Thomas, Sedberry and Bradley had grown up in the sandy, pine-covered hills of Moore County, but the sandy Carolina coast was completely different. They built and lived in crude houses on a thin island with the ocean on its south shore, an unbroken view of water that went on forever. Fort Macon claimed the eastern end of the island. Supplies had to be brought from the mainland across Bogue Sound on the north side.[9] The water was too shallow for boats, so the men waded out to carry back rations. Everything they did was accompanied by the sound of crashing waves and a salty breeze, which turned chilly through the fall.

Thomas worked on camp chores, guard duty, drilling and more drilling.[10] They practiced transitioning from column formation for movement to lines for battle. Although rifles would become more common as the war progressed, they still learned to attack in elbow-to-elbow lines, more effective for spreading short-range musket fire, to be followed by bayonet charge.[11] Thomas probably heard "Close the gap! Close the gap!" and firing orders in his sleep.

At times the drums would sound the long roll, on a rumor that the enemy was attacking, and the entire regiment would form up in lines. The first menace didn't come from the North, however, but from disease. With so many men who had never left home before living in one place, an epidemic of measles swept through the recruits. The sick were sent to a hospital established near Morehead City, but many still died.[12]

Col. Vance arrived and assumed command of the regiment. Corporal John R. Lane was elected captain. A couple of companies moved back to Morehead City, but Company H and the others settled in at Bogue Banks through November. Thomas and the other soldiers drilled and waited, wondering what this new war would bring next.[13]

CHAPTER 2
INHERITANCE

Archdale, Randolph County, North Carolina, ca. 1990

"I FOUND IT! IT WAS UNDER the bed." Oscar plopped a shallow cardboard box, like the kind that might hold stationery, onto the kitchen table. He shook the lid off as Mamaw, Papaw, Momma and I leaned forward to see. As he pulled out papers, I recognized the familiar gridlines of a family group sheet.

I'd taken a class in genealogy at the community college in southern Maryland, where I lived. Now on a weekend trip to my hometown in North Carolina, I had come over to my grandparents' house with Momma to visit. When I'd mentioned the class and started asking questions about the family, Uncle Oscar had started rummaging around in his bedroom.

Oscar pulled out a chair for me. I slid into it and studied the papers on the round formica table that took up most of their cozy kitchen. I'd heard the names of my great-grandparents, but didn't know all their children, when they were born, or where. What a treasure trove! I copied down everything onto one of my own blank forms the genealogy teacher had given me.

I carefully laid the family group sheet aside and looked at the next piece of paper. This one had no lines, just a little bit of writing on a blank sheet. A note at the top said these were Oscar's great-grandparents. Below that read:

> H) Thomas Maness believed to be from Arkansas
> left home before son was born (1875)
> told Pandora he was leaving to work in Bertha Zinc Mine in Virginia
> Frank Wiley went there at about 20 yrs old but couldn't find out anything.
> W) Sarah Pandora Wall (Walls)
> Frank Wiley b. 8 Aug 1875 Frank Shelley Community on Deep River, Guilford, N.C.
> married Emma[14]

I interpreted the abbreviations as "Husband" and "Wife." "Who's this?" I asked.

"That's Paw's mother and father," Papaw explained in his low, gravelly drawl. "Paw" was his father, Frank Wiley Maness, so this Thomas and Pandora were his grandparents.

"What's this about him going away to work?"

"Paw's daddy left in a buckboard wagon with some blankets. Said he was going to find work at the Bertha Zinc Mine, but he never come back."

"Did they ever find him?"

Papaw shook his head. "Nah. They never did."

I tried to wrap my mind around that. That was in the 1870s. Surely something had turned up since then.

Papaw had folded his lanky body into his usual chair between the window and the table. We all listened, rapt, as he continued, "When Paw was about 20, he went to the Bertha Zinc Mine, lookin' for his daddy. But nobody up there had heard anythin'."

"What about later? Did y'all look for him?" I asked.

"Paw carried a tintype picture around with him. He asked everybody if they'd seen him."

"There's a picture?!"

Papaw nodded.

Oscar asked, "Where is it, Daddy?"

"I don't remember. I'll look for it." He looked at Mamaw. "Do you know, Daisy?"

"Nah," she grunted. She couldn't speak well after a series of ministrokes, but she understood everything. They both promised to think about it. I learned later that Papaw had carried the picture around some after his father passed away, but not all the time. It must be a well worn picture to have lived in two generations' of wallets.

Momma said, "He could've fallen in a ditch somewhere and died. Nobody would've ever known who he was."

"You're right, Bessie," Oscar nodded.

"People didn't carry driver's licenses back then," she added.

I imagined the sad scene. If Thomas Maness had an accident and died on the road, he'd be a John Doe. Nobody who found him would even know how to contact his family.

On the way home, Momma told me her brother had dated a Mormon girl years ago. "Louise? I think her name was. Something like that. He should've married her. I thought they were serious." She chuckled, "Well, I guess not. Anyhow, she got him interested in genealogy."

I don't know when Oscar dated the Mormon lady, but he'd interviewed his grandmother to fill out the forms. Maw died when I was only two years old and I had no memory of her. My uncle had captured precious information and passed it along to me.

My thoughts returned to my mysterious great-great-grandfather. His family — his wife and then his grown son — had never found him when they were really looking. His grandson had asked everybody he'd ever met named Maness, and done no better.

I would probably never know what happened to Thomas Maness.

CHAPTER 3

INITIATION

Bogue Banks, N.C., November 1861

Thomas came under fire for the first time in early November. Company H and two other companies marched fifteen miles up the coast to salvage what they could from the wreck of the Federal steamer *Union*. Federal troops shot artillery at them, but no one was hurt.

Company H returned to Camp Wilkes on Bogue Banks November 16, and, in late November, they moved to the mainland with the rest of the regiment at winter quarters. In January, they boarded the train again and camped below New Bern to protect that town and its essential railroad.[15]

Thomas might have seen his brother that winter. Alexander "Sandy" Lane Maness had enlisted for the duration of the War on August 27, 1861, soon after Thomas signed up, also in Carthage. He couldn't read or write, but made it into the cavalry. He was about sixteen, but like Thomas, gave his age as eighteen.[16]

The Second Regiment North Carolina Cavalry was also called the Nineteenth Regiment N. C. Troops, to alleviate confusion with the Second Infantry. After forts along the Outer Banks fell to Federal troops, companies of the Nineteenth Regiment were sent to help

Col. Vance. Alexander, as part of Company I, spent part of the winter guarding the roads outside New Bern.[17] His company were all on horseback, but the whole regiment was shabbily armed, using pistols, muskets, shotguns — whatever came to hand — with a smattering of ammunition carried in their coat pockets or packs.[18]

Thomas and the rest of the North Carolina regiments, as part of Gen. L. O. Branch's brigade, camped about five miles south of New Bern. Men and defensive works stretched west from Fort Thompson — a strong fort with thirteen siege guns, ten field pieces, and three 32-pounders on the Neuse River — to the Weathersby Road near Bryce's Creek. The Atlantic and North Carolina Railroad cut through the middle of the Confederate line, about one and a half miles from Fort Thompson. The railroad, a brickworks, and irregular terrain left a gap in the Confederate fortifications. The army was working to rectify this, bringing in two 24-pounder guns.

Very late on March 12, 1862, Branch ordered the Twenty-Sixth down towards Otter Creek. They found the position already lost, the Yankees approaching more quickly than anticipated. Thomas and the Twenty-Sixth retreated back to their own defensive line, posted on the Confederate right, closest to Bryce's Creek. They had positioned artillery along the breastworks and cut down trees between them and the swamp, but Union forces arrived before everything was ready.[19]

Since Col. Vance was in charge of all the regiments west of the railroad, Lt. Col. Burgwyn commanded the Twenty-Sixth.[20] Knowing that many of the men had never fought before, he formed them up before the battle and addressed them. "Soldiers! the enemy are before you, and you will soon be in combat. You have the reputation of being one of the best drilled regiments in the service. Now I wish you to prove yourselves one of the best fighting. Men, stand by me, and I will by you."

The men all responded, "We will."[21]

Preparations continued into the morning of March 13. About 7:30 a.m., Thomas heard the thunder of Union gunboats firing from the Neuse River. Federals quickly broke through the weak point around the railroad and the brick kiln. They attacked the western portion, where the Twenty-Sixth and Thirty-Third North Carolina had a good position behind a creek, the forest having been cut down in front of that, and swamp to their right. The two sides exchanged fire for three hours.[22]

Burgwyn and the Twenty-Sixth kept fighting, not hearing until afternoon that the brigade was in retreat. In addition to casualties near the railroad, 150 men had been captured and Gen. Branch's couriers never made it to Vance's side. One captain barely escaped and reached Col. Vance about noon with the news. The enemy was moving up the railroad to flank him. Vance immediately ordered a retreat and sent word to Burgwyn on the right to follow.

Thomas, along with the rest of the regiment, crossed the Weathersby road and came up against Bryce's Creek and a scene of

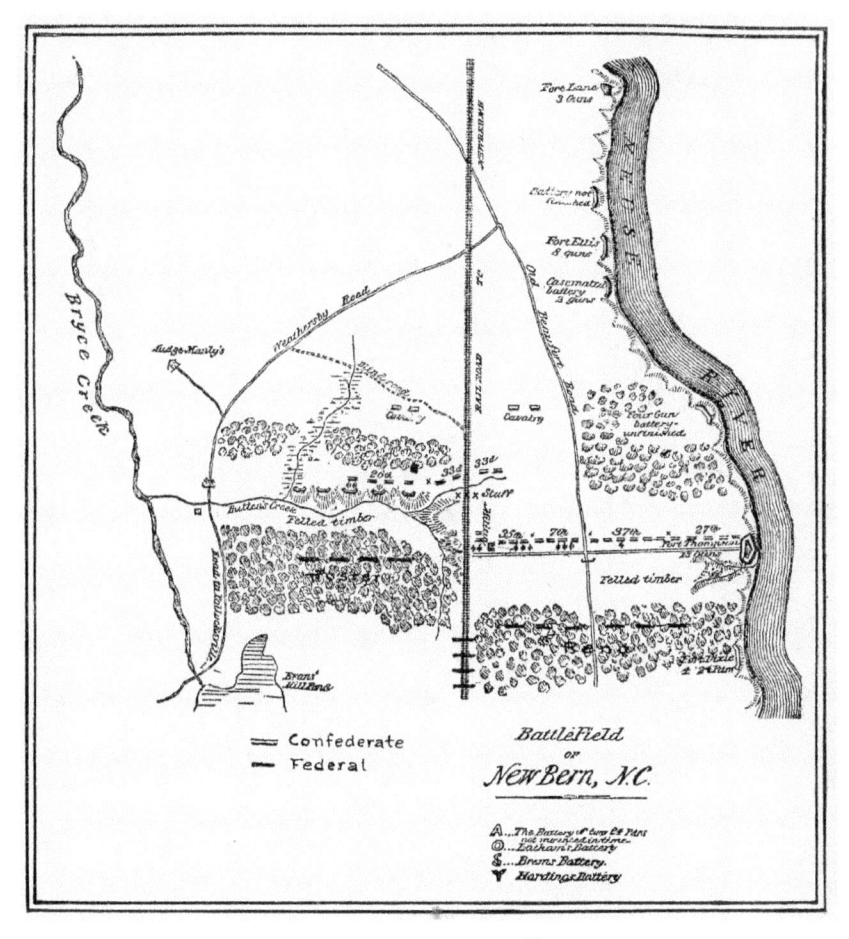

Battle of New Bern[23]

confusion. The bridge had been burnt and only one small boat was available, which could hold three men. The creek was deep and about seventy-five yards wide. On hearing the sound of artillery behind them, some men had jumped into the water and tried to swim across, but three had drowned in the strong current. Col. Vance had spurred his horse into the water, but fell off the thrashing animal and his gear dragged him under. Men on the other side had reached him and helped him to safety.[24]

The rest of the regiment was trapped.

CHAPTER 4
STARTING THE SEARCH

Washington, D.C. and Raleigh, N.C., 1991-1992

IN THE EARLY 1990S, ANY SERIOUS genealogy involved road trips, file drawers, microfilm and occasional letters. Having grown up in the kind of rural community where I could walk to a relative's house, writing letters to strangers intimidated me. I preferred travel, and the National Archives in Washington, D.C. was only two hours away from my home in southern Maryland, where I worked at the Patuxent River Naval Air Station.

So in March 1991, I ventured through the crazy D.C. traffic and found an after-hours parking spot. A National Archives assistant showed me how to use their soundex system to find Thomas Maness in the census records. Soundex was a way to find misspelled names by filing them according to consonant sounds. So "Maness" would turn into the alphanumeric code M520, which meant something like "M-N-S." I scrolled through the negative images on microfilm and found my great-grandfather as Franklin Maness, age 4, with his step-grandfather Gilbert Chappell and his mother Sarah P. Maness in the 1880 N.C. census.[25] I scribbled information in pencil onto blank census forms.

If Thomas were still alive in 1880, where was he? I checked the index and found many Thomas Manesses. Which one was mine? To narrow the search, I ruled out the Black families, assuming my family was always white. I didn't even know Thomas' birth date, only that he had a son in 1876. I looked for men who would have been at least in their 20s but no older than 40s that year. There were still too many. Some had other families; that couldn't be him, could it? Maybe he moved to another town, started another family and never came home. Just in case, I wrote down the entries who had children under 5 years old in 1880.

Maybe Thomas never even went to the Bertha Zinc Mine, but turned the horse as soon as he was out of sight and went somewhere else. Who was he? I had no birthdate, no parents, nothing except a huge window of estimated age. I took my pad of scribbles home, frustrated and tired.

Around 1992 I tried again, this time in Raleigh, at the North Carolina State Archives. I didn't have enough information to find Thomas in the census, but I did have an approximate marriage date. A marriage record might give his age. The librarian showed me to wide metal drawers of microfilm for each county. I threaded the film through the machine, turned on the light and began scrolling. The machine's fan whirred as I scanned the dark images: M, Mac, Mc, Mann... Maness.

Thomas S. Maness, married to Sarah P. Wall. The date was right. Pandora's first name was Sarah. I squinted at the scribbly negative on the screen. Martha Chappell had signed for her minor daughter. This was definitely the right family. I looked back up at the top. Thomas was 25! I looked again. Thomas' parents had been deceased, but he had given their names: George and Mary Maness.[26]

That gave me an estimated birth date, parents' names (so I thought), even a middle initial. I took an extra copy of the license to Papaw and Uncle Oscar (Mamaw had slipped away in her sleep in the spring of 1992). They had never seen it before, and were as excited as I was about the new details. Could this be the first new clue in our family mystery in the past century?

CHAPTER 5
CROSSING

Eastern North Carolina, 1862

As the three-man boat struggled across Bryce's Creek, many of the men panicked and threw their guns into the water, swearing the Yankees would never get them. Thomas was among the growing throng, along with three companies of the Nineteenth N.C. dismounted cavalry that had been guarding the Weathersby Road. Alexander was with the mounted companies retreating northward to find another crossing.[27]

Lt. Col. Burgwyn cooly ordered the confused troops into ranks. He sent a mounted company and the artillery off to save themselves, and gave his schoolmate, Lt. William A. Graham of the Nineteenth, a horse to scout the river. Burgwyn refused to get in the first boat, saying, "I will never cross until the last man of my regiment is over."[28]

By the time Graham returned to report the bridges had been set on fire, the men and Col. Vance, with the help of a slave on the opposite bank, had found three more boats, one of which would hold eighteen. Burgwyn and Graham counted off enough men for each boat and halted the column by crossing their swords across the path. It took four hours to ferry everyone across. About sunset, the two officers climbed aboard the last two boats, the sound of gunfire coming closer through the woods.[29]

Zebulon B. Vance[30]   *Henry K. Burgwyn Jr.*[31]   *William A. Graham*[32]

Col. Vance had taken a group and gone ahead towards Trenton with the Thirty-Third. Burgwyn ordered the men into formation. They marched through the night, joining up with the rest of the brigade in Trenton the following afternoon. Vance led the regiment on to Kinston. He later wrote, "We arrived at Kinston safely about noon on 16 March, having marched fifty miles in about thirty-six hours."[33]

They made it, but New Bern was lost. Five men of the Twenty-Sixth were killed, including a favorite officer, Maj. A. B. Carmichael. Capt. Martin of Company H also died. Ten were wounded and 72 captured or missing. All of the cavalry escaped. The Union forces had higher casualties, but the Confederates lost 150 prisoners in all.[34]

At Kinston, the Twenty-Sixth regrouped and resumed their routine of drill and practice. They eventually came under Brigadier-General Robert Ransom's brigade, along with five other North Carolina regiments.[35] First Lieutenant Clement Dowd was elected captain of Thomas' company to replace the fallen Capt. Martin.[36]

Lt. Col. Burgwyn had been very unpopular among the men before New Bern because of his strictness and constant drilling. They had even murmured threats about him among themselves. However, their first battle earned him new respect. The training and discipline, along with Burgwyn's coolness under fire, had overcome panic under enemy pursuit. Not only had he seen the last man into a boat before boarding himself, he followed up with the rear during the retreat to Trenton. Capt. Thomas J. Cureton wrote, "From this time on he had the entire confidence of his men and was their pride and love."[37]

In April, as the 12-month enlistments started coming due, Col. Vance encouraged southern patriotism and many, including Thomas Maness, re-enlisted for the duration of the war.[38] By that time, the North had taken all of coastal North Carolina except for Wilmington and Cape Fear.[39] On June 20, 1862, Ransom's brigade was ordered to Virginia to join Lee's army, which was fighting Union forces below Richmond.[40] Gen. Robert E. Lee had just taken command of the Confederate army, and he moved his "Army of Northern Virginia" to protect the southern capital from a threatening Federal force, known as the "Army of the Potomac," under Maj. Gen. George B. McClellan. Lee planned to strike that army, with the North Carolina Infantry as part of his plan.[41]

CHAPTER 6
CLUES AND STORIES

Robbins, Moore County, North Carolina, December 26, 1997

"Here's the road," Momma pointed. Oscar checked traffic and turned at the stop sign. Sitting in the middle in the cab of Oscar's pickup truck, I glanced down at the little sheet of notepaper, blue ballpoint scribble in my uncle's left-handed writing, and recited the next road to look for. We pulled into a driveway by a little white house and parked, looking around to see if any angry residents would run out and tell us we were in the wrong place. A woman appeared and opened the back screen door with a creak. "You found it! Come on in," she called.

She ushered us into the living room, where we met her husband and the object of our visit, Thurman Maness. He was tall, with large features and hands. The men shook hands and we all sat down, Momma and Oscar in the wing chairs across the room. I sank unexpectedly low in the well worn couch next to Mr. Maness, then scooted forward to balance on the edge. A spiral notebook lay across my lap, the few papers I had on Thomas Maness stuffed between the pages. Mrs. Maness brought us glasses of iced tea, the traditional Southern welcome for visitors. I sipped mine and set the glass on the short brown carpet, hoping I wouldn't forget and knock it over with my foot.

An acquaintance of Uncle Oscar's had touted Thurman as a guru on the Maness family. With a large binder opened across his lap, he started talking. William Maness came over from Scotland, and fought in the Revolutionary War. His son Billy had lots of children, including triplets named Shadrach, Meshach and Abednego.

Thurman reeled off names from memory, not looking at the pages on his lap. When I mentioned Thomas S. Maness, he laughed. "Thomas McSwain Maness. We called him Swain. He had five wives, and one of them was from Randolph County." Thurman only knew the name of his last wife, Sarah Brady. They married in 1901.

Randolph County! Could this be our Thomas, and his marriage to Pandora? I edged closer as he handed me the binder, generously telling me to copy whatever I wanted. As he chatted with Momma and Oscar, I wrote Swain Maness' basic genealogy as fast as I could. His father was Henry. Thurman didn't know who his mother was. Henry's father was Abednego, one of the triplets. If this was our man, we'd have Thurman's research to take us back to a family clan in Scotland!

Thurman rattled off stories as I copied notes. Swain was rumored to have killed a man in South Carolina, just so he could have the man's job. "They didn't want to bury him in the cemetery with the 'good folks,' so they buried him way out beyond the cemetery bounds." Thurman laughed. "And now the cemetery's grown so that he's in it with everybody else."

I didn't care much about siblings, cousins, or Civil War regiments at the time, but jotted down names and dates as my wrist began to ache. Most of Swain's and his siblings names rhymed: Thomas Swain (or McSwain, as Thurman thought), Alexander Lane, Shadrach Squire Gain, Lundy Jane, Leanda Cain, and Mary Kathryn (Catherine).

Thurman said he had met two of Swain's granddaughters a few years back, at a reunion or maybe a genealogical society meeting. They lived in Raleigh, he said.

I perked up. "What are their names?"

He shook his head. "I don't remember." He promised to check his notes to see if he could find them.

Could Swain Maness be our disappearing Thomas? It wasn't until later when I pored over my notes that I found problems. Swain's father was Henry, but Thomas' parents were George and Mary. Swain was born about 1833 — nobody knew the real date, but Thurman had guessed it from Swain's military record. Our marriage license set his birthdate around 1850, a huge difference. Could he have lied about his age when he married? I doubted a 37-year-old would have passed for a 25-year old.

I sat in the middle on the way home as we recounted some of the stories.

"I think it's him," said Oscar.

"Maybe," I answered. "One of his wives was from Randolph County."

"He had five wives!" Momma exclaimed.

"Do you count this as proof? Have we found our man?" Oscar asked as he drove and watched the road.

I shook my head. "It's promising. But the birthdate doesn't match. I still need proof."

Momma piped up. "I think we should dig him up and check his DNA!"

We all laughed. We'd heard of police using DNA to solve murder cases — on television, at least. They probably had special labs, lots of money to do that kind of thing. I imagined Thomas in his grave, dark brown bones in a decayed wooden casket. If Momma didn't mind, probably none of our family would mind desecrating her potential great-grandfather's grave. But this was 1997, and DNA analysis was way beyond regular folks like us, like science fiction. I settled back in my seat as the headlights illuminated the darkening road ahead of us. I would have to find some other way.

Thurman Maness (Courtesy of Lacy Garner Jr.)

CHAPTER 7
MALVERN HILL

Near Richmond, Virginia, June 24, 1862

THOMAS AND HIS FELLOWS RODE THE train to Petersburg. His older cousin, Ira Lane Maness, had joined Company H in March.[42] The whole brigade continued on to Richmond, with the Twenty-Sixth bringing up the rear and arriving June 25, 1862. Gen. Ransom immediately marched them down the Williamsburg Road, where the Twenty-Sixth relieved another regiment on picket duty, guarding the area from a nearby enemy unit.

As the evening grew darker, the men took their positions near a hedge on one side of a fence and settled in for the night. Suddenly, gunfire. Close. The Yankees were firing at them through the fence! They'd been there the whole time. The Twenty-Sixth had stumbled right up to them in the darkness.

Most of the regiment fled to the rear, but Companies G, H, and K held their lines and returned fire.[43] The other companies eventually returned, retaking the area. The regiment lost three men, with eight wounded.[44]

In the morning, the officers gave high compliments to Thomas' company and the men who held their ground, "undaunted by the nearness and numbers of the enemy," as described by the regiment's assistant surgeon, George Underwood.[45]

On June 27, the Twenty-Sixth took an unfinished barricade. When attacked later in the day, they successfully defended and kept the position. Meanwhile, about six miles to the north, Gen. Robert E. Lee and his Army of Northern Virginia had been fighting the Union army for two days. They pushed the Army of the Potomac across the Chickahominy River. With battles along the way, the Federals were retreating south, converging towards the North Carolina regiments.[46]

The Yankees took their stand July 1 at Malvern Hill, a gradual plateau that reached its height above craggy woods and the James River.[47] They set up a large battery of cannons near the foot of the hill, and the two armies fired at each other while building up their positions.

Gen. Ransom had refused several "orders" from Gen. Magruder to hurry to the front because Magruder was not in his chain of command. Finally, at about 7:00 p.m., with leeway from his commander, Gen. Huger, and another urgent request from Magruder, Ransom ordered the brigade into motion. As they "pushed forward under as fearful fire as the mind can conceive," according to Ransom,[48] soldiers from other brigades passed them in chaotic retreat. Burgwyn wrote that in their attempt to flank the enemy, the brigade was left unsupported in the confusion, and "the greater portion of the time the enemy's gunboats were shelling the field from which however the enemy suffered quite as much as we did." Several officers were wounded and one killed.[49]

After retreating from the front, Gen. Ransom quietly formed up his brigade in the woods to the west of the Union guns. The North Carolina regiments, including Thomas, used the rolling hills as cover to move quietly toward the federal guns in the dim twilight. The enemy seemed to be moving away from them, their attention on the battle at their front. Thomas and the others crept to within about 100 yards, seemingly unnoticed. Suddenly, they heard a poorly timed shout from another regiment in their brigade. "The enemy at once wheeled into line and opened upon us a perfect sheet of fire from muskets and the batteries," Ransom wrote. "We steadily advanced to within twenty yards

Battle of Malvern Hill, showing woods and hills on the western side, by Robert Knox Sneden [1862-1865][50]

of the guns. The enemy had concentrated his forces to meet us. Our onward movement was checked; the line wavered and fell back before a fire, the intensity of which is beyond description."[51]

Thomas and the other men lay on their bellies on the ground as shots flew over their heads. Flashes from the constant gunfire lit up everything. Dead and wounded men lay all around them.[52] Burgwyn wrote, "And how in the world I escaped I can only explain by ascribing the result to Providence. One shell burst immediately over me & solid shot struck not 3 feet from me, and the way the mini balls whistled was anything but pleasant."[53]

Finally they received the order to withdraw. Burgwyn gave the command, and they crawled back down the slope.[54] "It was a bitter disappointment to be compelled to yield when their guns seemed almost in our hands." wrote Gen. Ransom.[55]

Peter Ellis, an eighteen-year-old in the Thirteenth Mississippi, wrote of the battlefield, "As the roar of musketry, the boom of cannon, the bursting shells and hissing grapeshot slowly subsided the shrieks of the wounded could be heard on every hand. Fervent prayers, bitter swearing, pitiful calls for water and for comrades by name or company were among the cries distinguishable. As the dense smoke, which had obscured everything, slowly lifted the setting sun as red as blood could be seen, and the surface of the earth as far as I could see appeared to be covered with a mass of wriggling, writhing men, some vainly endeavoring to regain their feet, others seeking less painful positions. Intermixed with the wounded everywhere lay the silent forms of the dead, men of the gray and of the blue."[56]

Wounded men called out in the night, saying their regiment name as they groaned for help. A detail was organized to find and remove any of the Twenty-Sixth's men. Hundreds of Union dead were left behind for the Confederate army to burn or bury.[57] The agonizing cries of dying men haunted the survivors. Killing them would be a mercy.

By morning, a chill rain settled in, making the field even more slippery and adding to the survivors' misery. Burgwyn slept propped against a fence.[58] Capt. John Lane of Company G slept between two of his soldiers. He woke in the morning to find them both dead, hit by enemy fire in their sleep.[59]

Although the Union army retreated back across the river the next day, leaving Richmond in relative safety, Confederate losses were high, with more than 5,000 dead from the final day at Malvern Hill and 20,000 dead from the Seven Days campaign. After the battle, officers and probably the men realized that the attack had not gone at all as planned, with one regiment going the wrong direction and not arriving until late, and other groups mistaking a defensive battle cry for the signal for everybody to attack, despite the artillery not being in place.[60]

CHAPTER 8

DESERTERS

Richmond, Va., 1862-1863

AFTER MALVERN HILL, THE SOLDIERS' IDEAS about the glories of war dissipated like fog on a sunny morning. Not only had they reenlisted for the duration of the war — which now seemed farther off than it had before — a conscription act had been passed, forcing non-volunteers to serve in the Confederate army. Ira Maness deserted in August 1862. Another of Thomas' cousins, Isaac Maness Jr., hated taking orders and deserted several times, finally returning to Moore County for good in the spring of 1863.[61]

Soldiers that had gone Absent Without Leave — to see family members, for example — and returned had been treated mercifully. When eleven members of Company B deserted in December 1862, however, the sergeant of the group was court-martialed and condemned to be shot. As he knelt blindfolded in front of the firing squad, a pardon arrived with seconds to spare and he lived to fight in future battles.[62]

That August, in 1862, Col. Vance was elected as Governor of North Carolina. He had always been popular with the men, who were sad to see him leave. Gen. Ransom's disapproval of Henry Burgwyn's promotion to colonel led to the regiment's transfer to Brig. Gen. James

J. Pettigrew's Brigade, all North Carolina regiments. Pettigrew and Burgwyn were fellow alumni of the State University (University of North Carolina) and had similar temperament and military style. Capt. John R. Lane was promoted to lieutenant colonel in Burgwyn's place, and John T. Jones promoted to major. Lt. H. C. Albright became captain of Company H.[63]

Now in Richmond, the Twenty-Sixth continued to drill, the officers proud of the regiment's reputation for discipline and efficiency. Through early 1863, Thomas moved with his regiment to different stations around Richmond and eastern North Carolina. In March, an attack on Federal gun boats near New Bern failed when one of the brigade's Parrott guns burst and defective ammunition endangered the men on the other two guns. Gen. Pettigrew, despite having to order retreat, commended the men. "In seven days they marched 127 miles; waded swamps, worked in them by night and day, bivouaced in the rain, some times without fire, never enjoyed a full night's rest after the first, besides undergoing furious shelling, and discharging other duties."[64]

After winning a battle at little Washington, a fortified town in North Carolina, the brigade had to retreat again as Union gunboat reinforcements arrived. The losses, long marches, scanty rations, and swamps wore on the men. Passing through towns that had been destroyed lowered morale. On May 1, 1863, the brigade received the order to move back into Virginia with enthusiasm at the thought of leaving the skirmishes for a real fight against the Yankees. By that afternoon, the men of the Twenty-Sixth were riding in the train cars. In Virginia, Pettigrew's brigade became part of the Gen. Lee's Army of Northern Virginia.[65] On May 8, the Twenty-Sixth finally received something Burgwyn had been asking for: a brand new battle flag.[66]

CHAPTER 9
SHADRACH

Moore County, January 1863

Not all of Thomas' family had been excited to join the army, even in the initial excitement. His brother, Shadrach Squire Gain Maness, was still living in Moore County when the Confederate Congress passed the Conscription Act.

When the orphaned siblings were farmed out to different family members, Alexander and little sister Mary Catherine had been taken in by Ira Maness, who lived in Prosperity, in the northern part of Ritters Township, Moore County. Shadrach was taken in by Quimby Wallace, in the Gold Region, farther south in Sheffields township. The draft didn't target 15-year-old Shadrach, but took aim at 30-year-old Quimby, a farmer with a young family.

Shadrach must have become fond of Quimby and Arabella, who had provided him a home, and their two small children, William and Martha, ages about 5 and 4. How could these little ones survive without their father to work the large farm? Quimby did not own slaves and Shadrach was the only non-family member living with them in 1860.[67] There were only two ways to avoid conscription: pay a $500 fine — so the rich didn't have to fight — or send a substitute. Shadrach volunteered to go as Quimby's replacement. On January

27, 1863, he went to Carthage and made his mark, claiming to be sixteen.[68]

Having signed up for a three-year enlistment, he joined Company D of the Forty-Ninth North Carolina Infantry in Goldsboro or Kenansville as they rested from the fighting in Virginia. On February 22, Shadrach rode with the other soldiers in flatcars on the train to Wilmington, North Carolina. In late March, they took the train again to Goldsboro.[69]

Since the Forty-Ninth had formed in April 1862, the men had nearly a year of training and battle experience. They had also survived that initial onslaught of measles and other diseases that spread among so many men living together, combined with little knowledge of sanitation or germs. Now, it was Shadrach's turn. He became sick and was reported to be in the hospital from March through June 1863. Whatever he had, it affected him for months. He was finally sent home on furlough to recover, through at least August and maybe into the fall.[70]

CHAPTER 10

ALEXANDER

Culpepper County, Virginia, June 8, 1863

Since the Battle of New Bern in March 1862, Thomas' other brother, Alexander Maness, had spent the past year "on picket," or guard duty, first in North Carolina and later in Virginia, with the exception of skirmishes and protecting Gen. Lee's flank in the Battle of Fredericksburg in December.[71] In November the Nineteenth Regiment N. C. Troops (Second Regiment N. C. Cavalry) had been attached to the Army of Northern Virginia in Gen. W. H. F. Lee's Brigade, part of the Cavalry Corps under Gen. J. E. B. "Jeb" Stuart.[72] They had spent the winter picketing the Rappahannock River in Virginia.[73]

W. A. Graham, a captain in another company of Alexander's regiment, described patrol duty: "A company of from thirty to sixty men would go from twenty to twenty-five miles to the front, establish its picket in from a half to a fourth of a mile of those of the enemy, who had a 'reserve' of several thousand a mile or two in their rear. ... Each company in turn had a picket tour of about ten days on one of the roads, and frequently the horses were not unsaddled for half that time. It frequently rained nearly every day of the ten. Consequently, three-fourths of the horses returned from picket with sore backs. The regiment was armed with almost every kind of arms (except the newest patterns) known to the warrior or sportsman, and was never fully equipped with arms of modern warfare until it equipped itself with those furnished by the United States and taken from its troops in Virginia." Graham writes of his company's pickets with about thirty-five men and a mix of carbines, double-barreled shotguns, six-shooters, a handful of rifles and old "one-barrel 'horse pistols.'" Carbines were shorter-barrel muskets or rifles. Ammunition was scarce, with some carrying a few handfuls of rounds in their clothes or haversacks. He wrote, "Was not this a 'formidable array' to place itself within ten miles of the headquarters of thirty thousand men equipped with arms of modern pattern?"[74]

Ammunition wasn't the only scarcity. A clerk for Company E of the brigade wrote about his company in March 1863, of "horses dying with starvation and the men doing but little better." Nevertheless, the cavalry's job was to observe the fords on the Rappahannock and distract the enemy from the main army. Alexander and his fellows not only harassed the Union forces, they poked and prodded and reported back to Gen. Robert E. Lee on their movements.[75]

The brigade had been camping near Brandy Station in Virginia since March. Col. Solomon "Sol" Williams, just returned as a newly-wed, had taken command of the Second N.C. Cavalry on June 1. A railroad ran along the plain between Brandy Station and Culpepper Courthouse. On Monday, June 8, 1863, the regiment marched and galloped about the plain in a grand review of the Cavalry Corps for Gen. Robert E. Lee. They were planning to go on picket at another spot on the Rappahannock River the next morning.[76]

About 6:30 a.m. on June 9, Alexander woke to "Saddle Up," a nickname they'd given to the "Boots and Saddles" call because so many of them lacked boots. About a half hour later Col. Williams had them mount up and form "column of fours." They began to gallop as they reached the road towards Beverly Ford. This was not a normal picket, but most of the men didn't know what was going on. More than a mile up the road, they cleared the woods as a shell cut off the top of a nearby tree. They had been harassing the Union army on the other side of the river, distracting the enemy from Lee's movements toward the north. But today, Gen. Alfred Pleasanton's Cavalry Corps and two brigades of infantry had crossed the fords before daylight, bringing the attack to them.

The Second N.C. galloped past a house and splashed through Ruffin's Run, then took position behind a hill with the Tenth Virginia, which had set up two horse-drawn guns. Col. Williams ordered the men with rifles — probably including Alexander — to dismount and move to the front, firing on the enemy, who had also dismounted and taken position behind a stone wall about 300 yards in front of them.[77]

Williams ordered a charge. The men stormed ahead, on foot. Alexander saw several men in the other companies fall. They took the wall, capturing eighteen prisoners plus some wounded. They held the wall until 2:00 p.m., when Gen. W. H. F. Lee moved the brigade back across the ridge, forming up with other regiments across the plain of Fleetwood Hill. Federal forces that had crossed at Kelly's Ford began driving into two other Virginia regiments on their left. Col. Williams galloped past the Virginians to the Second N.C. and formed them up by squadron. As the Tenth Virginia fired past their pressed compatriots, the Second N.C. charged around them with sabers drawn, cutting into enemy cavalry and infantry. They drove them back about

Cavalry Charge Near Brandy Station, Virginia by Edwin Forbes (1864)[78]

half a mile into their reserve forces, which were posted on a hill. Then those reserves shot a volley which stopped them.

Col. Williams was reforming the regiment when a shot through the head killed him. Artillery fire from the right poured into them and they fell back, keeping formation. The Union cavalry tried to charge, but the North Carolinians fired on them and they fell back again. Graham wrote, "In the charge, we relieved a great many of our dismounted men, who had fallen into the hands of the enemy, and also a gun of the horse artillery...."[79] At some point, though, Alexander was captured and apparently not one of those freed by the charge.[80]

Union forces eventually "retired" after the all-day battle, the largest cavalry clash of the war. Meanwhile, Alexander was taken to Old Capitol Prison in Washington, D.C. Later in June, he was moved with other prisoners to City Point, a growing port town on the Appomattox River that connected ships from the north to Virginia railroads.[81]

★ ★ ★

With the cavalry screening their movements, Thomas' regiment and the rest of the Army of Northern Virginia began to move north. The war still dragged on, and Gen. Robert E. Lee knew the North had more resources and seemingly endless manpower. The presence of the Confederate army drained supplies in the South wherever they camped. Lee looked to the North not only for victory, but also for resources from prosperous lands that would give their own civilians and farms a break.[82]

In early June, the army moved out toward the Shenandoah Valley and northward. They spread out, with the Twenty-Sixth bringing up the rear to protect Richmond and Fredericksburg as long as possible. When they spotted an empty camp from which the Feds had been firing on them the day before, their officers knew their movements had been discovered. It was time to head north and join the rest of the army. The men of the Twenty-Sixth cooked up their rations and began to march on June 15, 1863, their wagons of supplies behind them.[83]

It was a long, hard march up through Virginia. Low on gear, some of the men tackled roads, woods, and swamps barefoot. They finally crossed the Potomac River and caught up with the rest of Lee's army in southern Pennsylvania. The farms and fields looked lush, and they commandeered cattle and crops to feed the troops. However, the commanders enforced a strict policy of not looting the citizens, as in not stealing shop goods or destroying crops. Despite the harsh treatment the Union had given citizens in the South, they wanted to gain the sympathies of the civilians. One soldier recalled, "The farmers along our line of march were quietly reaping and housing their grain. They did not seem to be in the least frightened or dismayed by our presence, and were left by us in the quiet and undisturbed possession of their crops."[84]

The Moore County boys had seen all kinds of land since they'd left the sandy pine woods of home: the coast, the swamps and rivers of eastern North Carolina, mountains and forests, and now, the large, plentiful farms of Pennsylvania. It must have looked like a paradise, bursting with acres of crops coming into harvest.[85]

They stopped and had Sunday services on June 28, 1863. On June 30, as Alexander was being exchanged as one of 858 Confederate prisoners of war at City Point, the Twenty-Sixth reached a small town in Pennsylvania, Cashtown. Appropriate to its name, officers mustered all the men, taking roll and paying out the bimonthly payroll of $11 a month. The regiment then marched a few more miles and set up camp "in a beautiful grove" by a little creek with a stone bridge, less than four miles from Gettysburg.[86]

CHAPTER 11
GETTYSBURG

West of Gettysburg, Pennsylvania, July 1, 1863

Early in the morning of July 1, 1863, the brigade moved out towards Gettysburg. The day before, Gen. Pettigrew had taken three regiments toward the town "to procure shoes and other army supplies for his men," but ran into Union cavalry and returned after a skirmish.[87] The generals disagreed on whether this purported a small Federal station or part of the larger army. Not knowing exactly what was up ahead, Gen. Lee sent out Heth's Division of infantry.[88]

The Twenty-Sixth, as part of Pettigrew's North Carolinians, marched in the rear with Brockenborough's Virginians, following the Tennessee and Mississippi brigades. They could hear small arms fire ahead. Reaching the top of a hill, they took position behind the batteries. As they waited, artillery fire occasionally reached them, killing and wounding some of the men. Col. Burgwyn rode along the line, calling, "Steady boys, steady," and the seeds of panic faded.[89]

Finally receiving the command from Pettigrew, Burgwyn ordered, "March!" The regiments quickly spread out into battle-line formation, with the Twenty-Sixth on the left. They halted in a woods. Maj. John T. Jones wrote, "In our front was a wheat-field about a fourth of a mile wide; then came a branch (Willoughby Run), with thick underbrush and briars skirting the banks. Beyond this again was an open field with the exception of a wooded hill (McPherson's woods) directly in front of the Twenty-sixth Regiment, and about covering its front."[90]

They lay impatiently in the woods, harassed by occasional sniper fire, waiting for the other brigades to take position. They could see the enemy in the woods beyond the branch, about 300 yards distant, regiments with high-crowned black hats — the "Iron Brigade," the Nineteenth Indiana and the Twenty-fourth Michigan regiments.[91]

About 2:00 p.m., the orders "Attention" and then "Forward March" were given. The men obediently stood up and moved out, knowing full well they were out in the open. The enemy opened fire, but the men kept in step and in line, as they had drilled so many times. Company H was not the closest to the flag, but as part of the regiment they "dressed on the colors," using it to keep formation. The rest of the division moved in staggered lines behind and beside them, a wave of infantry nearly a mile long.[92]

Formation broke in the briars and brambles in the ravine of Willoughby's Run. Artillery from the right side of the woods poured into them as well as infantry fire. Those who made it across the creek quickly formed up again and returned fire as they pushed up the slope, yelling the "Rebel yell," a high, throaty call that might have been influenced by American Indian war cries. Union Col. Henry Morrow described the Twenty-Sixth's advance as, "... They came on in rapid strides yelling like demons."[93]

A prime target, the Twenty-Sixth's flag had already fallen ten times, the color guard all killed or wounded.[94] As bullets and shells decimated the two companies on either side of the flag, the others moved inward to fill the gaps.[95] After bringing a message of praise from Pettigrew to Burgwyn, Capt. McCreery took the flag and moved forward. A shot immediately pierced his heart. He fell, covering the flag in blood.

Lt. George Wilcox of Company H rushed forward. He pulled the flag from under McCreery, raised it and walked a few steps. A shot in his right side slowed him. Another shot in his left foot brought him to the ground.[96]

Underwood writes, "The line hesitates; the crisis is reached; the colors must advance." Col. Burgwyn tells Lt. Col. Lane the words of praise received from Gen. Pettigrew, then takes the flag himself. "Dress on the colors," he orders. A private comes to take the flag but as Burgwyn turns to hand it to him, he "is hit by a ball on the left side, which, passing through both lungs, the force of it turns him around and, falling, he is caught in the folds of the flag and carries it with him to the ground." The brave private also dies a moment later.[97]

Lane gives orders to the right and left sides of the regiment to advance, then returns and takes up the flag. A lieutenant tells him, "No man can take these colors and live."

> Lane replies, "It is my time to take them now"; and advancing with the flag, shouts at the top of his voice: "Twenty-sixth, follow me." The men answer with a yell and press forward. Several lines of the enemy have given away, but a most formidable line yet remains, which seems determined to hold its position. Volleys of musketry are fast thinning out those left and only a skeleton line now remains. To add to the horrors of the scene, the battle smoke has settled down over the combatants making it almost as dark as night. With a cheer the men obey the command to advance, and rush on and upward to the summit of the hill, when the last line of the enemy gives way and sullenly retires from the field through the village of Gettysburg to the heights beyond the cemetery.
>
> When about thirty steps distant, as Colonel Lane turns to see if his regiment is following him, a ball fired ... strikes him in the back of the neck just below the brain, which crashes through his jaw and mouth, and for the fourteenth and last time the colors are down."[98]

Maj. Jones led the remnant with muskets and bayonets to push the Union lines back on each other. He writes, "On this second line, the fighting was terrible — our men advancing, the enemy stubbornly resisting, until the two lines were pouring volleys into each other at a distance not greater than 20 paces. At last the enemy were compelled to give way."[99] Other brigades finally arrived, pushing the Federals in a gradual retreat to Seminary Ridge. Both sides retired for the night, preceding two more days of bloody battle.[100]

The Twenty-Sixth Regiment suffered terrible losses at Gettysburg. They started with 800 officers and men. Only 216 returned unscathed the first day, with a loss of 584 killed or wounded. Regimental losses were "the greatest in numbers and greatest in per cent ... of all the regiments on either side in the Civil War in any one battle."[101] Another 130 men were lost on the third day. "Our total loss in battle, then, was 588 killed and wounded, and 126 missing" — nearly ninety percent.[102] The retreating regiment, charged with guarding the artillery after the battle, consisted of 67 privates and three officers, not counting extra-duty men such as cooks, some of whom had been armed after the first day.[103]

Thomas' relatives and friends were among the casualties. On the first day of the battle, a bullet ripped through Sedberry's jaw. Someone dragged him to a roadside with other wounded and dying men.[104] Bradley Brady was shot in the thigh and arm. Both men were taken to the Union hospital in Gettysburg, simultaneous salvation and capture.[105]

But where was Thomas Maness?

CHAPTER 12

SURVIVOR

Petersburg, Virginia, 1863

Thomas never made it to Pennsylvania. As his company splashed through Willoughby's Run in the charge up McPherson's hill, Thomas bided in a hospital back in Petersburg. He had spent many months before that in prison.

Thomas had been present and accounted for through the end of October 1862. By late December, he was in prison in Petersburg. The only record, a note by his name on Company H's muster rolls, doesn't specify a reason. Perhaps he tried to desert with his Moore County companions and got caught. Ira Maness had successfully escaped in August 1862. Isaac Maness, who seemed to come and go as he pleased, would desert for the final time the following spring. Privates Robert Cox and B. G. Lewis had deserted the company in December 1862 and January 1863, respectively.[106]

Thomas might have been held in the old trading post, a two-story stone house that had belonged to Peter Jones, colonial namesake of Petersburg. Before they had many prisoners of war, the building "was used for miscreant Confederate soldiers."[107] Whatever Thomas did, he was lucky to escape a firing squad. He remained in prison through at least the end of April 1863.[108]

Release and return to duty were the last things Thomas wanted. According to stories passed down in the family, he would get a "bad feeling" before a particularly brutal battle. He would procure a laxative from the dispensary, then take an extra dose of "the salts." Dysentery was deadly throughout the war; with similar symptoms, Thomas would be rushed to the hospital and would certainly be unable to fight. Truly "lucky" patients might be discharged and sent home. Sometime in May or June, 1863, Thomas had a long stay in the hospital in Petersburg.[109]

Although several factories had been converted into hospitals, Thomas most likely stayed in the camp hospital in Poplar Lawn Park, a former mustering ground also called "The Lawn." Sick and wounded Confederate soldiers, especially North Carolina troops, were treated there that year.[110] Although alive and safe, Thomas' insides probably felt as bad as a gut-shot soldier on the front line. He wasn't lucky enough to get a discharge, but he managed to survive Gettysburg, as few in his company did. With 17 killed and 55 wounded in the battle, Company H had been reduced from seventy-eight to just six active-duty men.[111]

The remnants of Thomas' company and the rest of the Army of Northern Virginia limped back to Orange County Courthouse in upper Virginia. The exhausted men had retreated through lower Pennsylvania in depressing rain and mud. Union cavalry attacked the wagons, slowed by muddy roads. Lt. Col. Lane, who had miraculously survived, escaped by slipping out of a wagon of wounded men and mounting his horse. He could neither speak nor eat for nine days, his throat and mouth swollen and inflamed. The other officers thought he would die.[112] Gen. Pettigrew was fatally wounded in the skirmish with the cavalry and died in Virginia. Hundreds of men of the rear guard were trapped on the wrong side of the Potomac River and captured after a pontoon bridge was cut to keep it from falling into the hands of the enemy.[113]

Thomas was in and out of active duty during the following months. He was admitted to the Wayside Hospital in Richmond October 9, 1863. The following day, he was transferred to Winder Hospital.[114] His "illness" came just in time — Lee's army, still north of Richmond around Orange County Courthouse, marched out on October 9. A few days later they attacked the rear of the Union army at Bristoe Station, when another unit ambushed them. More men were killed and wounded, including those in the Twenty-Sixth Regiment, with no clear winner. Even Gen. Kirkland, who had taken over Pettigrew's Brigade, was wounded.[115]

Thomas had escaped another useless blood bath. But he couldn't stay in the hospital forever.

CHAPTER 13

FROM THE FIRE INTO THE FRYING PAN

Virginia, 1863-1864

In mid-November 1863, despite having sixty more days of leave because of his injury, Lt. Col. Lane visited the men of the Twenty-Sixth. He wrote, "I found the regiment so low in spirits and few in number that the day I reached camp, was, I believe, the saddest day to me of all the war." He attributed his men's low morale to the many losses of their friends, as well as Col. Burgwyn and Gen. Pettigrew. "Regretting so much to see the gallant old regiment go down, notwithstanding the fact that I was entirely unable for active service, I reported myself for duty...."[116] He was made full colonel, in charge of the Twenty-Sixth, backdated to the battle of Gettysburg.

Maj. John T. Jones was promoted to lieutenant colonel. The higher-ups tried to merge the reduced regiment into another group, but Lane lobbied and won, to have their Twenty-Sixth remain its own entity. He used drill, music from Capt. Mickey's band, and keeping the regiment intact to rebuild their morale and regimental pride.[117]

Sedberry Maness and Bradley Brady both had survived the Battle of Gettysburg. After being treated in the Union hospital, they were sent to the prison camp on David's Island, New York. A couple of months later, they were exchanged at City Point, Virginia. Sedberry and Bradley returned to duty by mid-February 1864, despite their severe wounds. The regiment issued them new clothes on February 13.[118]

Thomas must have joined the troops at Orange Courthouse by winter. He mustered and received his pay December 31. He made his mark on a receipt for new clothes, issued in February or March 1864.[119]

Meanwhile, Alexander Maness and the rest of the Second N. C. Cavalry had protected the infantry's flanks at Bristoe Station and had engaged Federal cavalry at nearby places in Virginia throughout the fall. Both armies settled into "winter quarters," with cavalry units picketing the Rapidan River. Alexander was captured near the river on February 7, 1864.[120] On February 11, he was sent to Old Capital Prison in Washington, D.C.[121]

Gen. Grant's Army of the Potomac crossed the Rapidan River on May 4, 1864. Gen. Lee sent two corps to meet them, and the Twenty-Sixth marched at the head of the Kirkland's brigade (Kirkland had recovered). The armies clashed on May 5, cavalry first and then the infantry. Southern forces drove the Northern army back, fighting in a dense wood called the Wilderness. Col. Lane was wounded in the thigh, leaving Lt. Col. Jones in command of the Twenty-Sixth. That night they camped, expecting to be relieved by another corps. But the Federals surprised them at 5:00 a.m. with a violent attack, thirteen brigades against eight. Jones rallied his men and led a charge, but was severely wounded. When he asked, Assistant Surgeon W. W. Gaither told him the wound was mortal; "... with a yearning expression [Jones] replied: 'It must not be. I was born to accomplish more good than I have done.'"[122]

Col. Lane returned to duty despite his leg. The brigade held their lines, with the Twenty-Sixth positioned in the middle. A member of one of its companies said they "fought until not a cartridge was left."[123] Longstreet's relief corps arrived in an orderly march and pushed Grant's forces back. They would have pursued, but one of his own men accidentally shot Gen. Longstreet.

FROM THE FIRE INTO THE FRYING PAN 49

The two armies moved like chess pieces around upper Virginia through the rest of May. In early June, at the battle of Cold Harbor, success of the battle went back and forth between the two armies. By the third day, Gen. Kirkland had been wounded but more than 12,000 Union men had fallen.[124]

Thomas had survived yet another bloody battle. The past two summers had brought devastating bloodshed, which he had witnessed at Malvern Hill and where he had lost many fellows at Gettysburg. The anniversary of those battles was coming soon. What horror would this year bring? He couldn't keep feigning sickness. Some of his cousins had deserted, but home was far away, on foot, and if he were caught again he could be shot. Alexander was a prisoner. Sedberry and Bradley had been wounded, taken prisoner, exchanged, and thrown right back into it. Bradley had a wife and son back home. Both he and Thomas wanted out.[125]

Grant's and Lee's armies began converging toward the James River June 12-13 — without Thomas. On June 10, just northeast of Richmond, he slipped away from the regiment. He made his way to a Union Camp in Chickahominy and turned himself in. Later records claimed that he tried to join the Union army. He probably hoped, at worst, to be sent to prison in D.C. where he could see Alexander.[126]

Things didn't quite work out according to plan. Wary of Confederate deserters as potential spies, Union soldiers took Thomas prisoner and sent him to the Camp Hoffman prison camp at Point Lookout, Maryland.[127]

CHAPTER 14
GHOST STORIES

Point Lookout, Maryland, ca. October 1990

T̲HE POINT LOOKOUT LIGHTHOUSE WAS OPEN to the public for the first time in over a century. I "collected" lighthouses, in that I visited one whenever I got the chance or wherever I traveled. Point Lookout was down at the end of the Southern Maryland peninsula, where the Potomac River empties into the Chesapeake Bay. On a clear day, you can see the shoreline of Virginia across the water.

I made it to the lighthouse in the afternoon, just before closing time. Guest storytellers, who remembered the lighthouse keepers, had already left. I was ushered inside to look around on my own, but encouraged to be quick about it as the park ranger waited near the door to lock up.

The house was bare, emptied of furnishings or decoration. I climbed up into the cupola and looked around. It, too, was bare, the fresnel lens having been removed. I still had that feeling of satisfaction, having been in it,

Point Lookout Lighthouse, south side (facing water), ca. 1990

as if checking off another item for my collection. The waters of the Chesapeake were dark blue under a sunny sky, but I didn't have time to savor the view. I waited for a man and his daughter to look around and finally climb back down, so I could take a quick photo without obstructions. Then I hurried back through the house and followed the ranger out the front door.

As we descended the steps, she pointed to a doorway beneath the porch. "That's the basement. People always want to see that."

I peered inside, smelling the damp, cool air of concrete and dirt that never see the sun. "Why?" I asked.

"The ghosts!" she laughed. At my blank expression, she asked, "You haven't heard about the ghosts?" She gestured along the road and her tone grew more serious. "All this was a prisoner-of-war camp during the Civil War. Hundreds of men died here. Some say their spirits roam Point Lookout at night."

Point Lookout Lighthouse, north side, ca. 1990

"Hunh."

"A lot of the stories are here at the lighthouse. Researchers come here to get tape recordings in the basement." She shrugged as she locked the gate behind us. "They say they don't hear anything, but then get voices on the tape recordings."

"Voices! What do they say?"

"I don't know. Just talking, I guess."

I walked around and took a couple of pictures of the lighthouse, zooming in on the empty cupola. I took all ghost stories with a big grain of salt, believing that people experienced unexplainable phenomena but not necessarily that it emanated from dead people.

I drove away with the window down, enjoying the salty breeze as I passed beaches, piers, and mostly woods. Most of my ancestors that I knew about were Quakers, who wouldn't have been involved in wars. On a high-school trip to Gettysburg, Pennsylvania, years ago, I'd found the battlefields empty and boring and the huge graveyards with anonymous, identical stones depressing. I wasn't interested in ghosts, and I had absolutely no interest in the Civil War.

View of Point Lookout Lighthouse from the west side of the peninsula, where the Potomac River enters the Chesapeake Bay (all from author's collection)

CHAPTER 15
PRISONER OF WAR

Point Lookout, Maryland, June 24, 1864

Thomas arrived on Friday, June 24, a hot, oppressive day. The multi-winged Hammond General Hospital, near the lighthouse, dominated the end of the Point Lookout peninsula. Farther east, on the Chesapeake Bay shore, guards put Thomas inside Camp Hoffman's massive, wood-fenced enclosure. He saw acres of tents, row upon row, the only shelter for prisoners. Any hopeful look at the six long buildings would soon be disappointed; they were mess halls that could serve five hundred men at the time.[128]

As President Lincoln and Gen. Grant had banned prisoner exchanges by August 1863, and the Battle of Gettysburg added an influx of prisoners, small prison camps that had formerly been hospitals or garrisons quickly overflowed. Smallpox raged through the camp. Crowded conditions, brackish wells and shortage of rations contributed to about twelve to fifteen deaths per day.[129]

Some of the prisoners could write, and did. Charles Warren Hutt, a Virginian, kept a diary. He went swimming to cool off on the day Thomas arrived and didn't notice any new arrivals. On Saturday, July 2, he wrote about the arrival of the Second Massachusetts Cavalry, a

Black regiment. He also mentioned, "Several hundred prisoners left for Elmira New York today. Others expected to follow."[130]

Ex-slaves stood duty as guards, sometimes shooting randomly into the camp. A "wall of death" kept prisoners from approaching within 10 feet of the stockade, or wooden fence, because those who did became target practice. Another fellow prisoner, Walter D. Addison, recalled, "During my entire confinement at Point Lookout we were under guard of Negro soldiers whose conduct and treatment of the prisoners was infamously cruel and in many instances they conducted themselves in a savage manner. I have witnessed them fire their muskets indiscriminately into crowded masses of prisoners, shooting two or three men at a single shot, and such outrages were tolerated by their white officers … and I never heard that one was even reprimanded." Addison adds that the post office was watched, or rather, letters were extremely censored so that no word could get out about conditions in the camp.[131]

The water was constantly there, but none of it good to drink. Thomas and the other prisoners could bathe in the water as long as no one ventured far from shore. The thin line of land on the horizon enticed them — Virginia, the South. A strong swimmer could make it; a desperate inland boy could try. But the guards watched them all the time, even at night, and the water wouldn't stop a ball.

On the hottest days, the distant coastline of Virginia disappeared. The heavy haze blended water and sky so you couldn't tell where one stopped and the other began. Steamboats churned up and down the Potomac. On July 4, gunboats in the river, decorated with flags, fired salutes. Sickness and deaths continued. More prisoners were sent to Elmira.

Hutt wrote on July 14, "From one thousand to twelve hundred prisoners went out this morning and took the Oath of Allegiance to the W. states."[132] If Thomas deserted to the enemy as his record says, he was probably eager to take the oath and be set free, or even sent as a soldier out West. If so, he must have felt cheated that so many men were freed and he continued to be overlooked.

After a month in this oppressive place, Thomas might have been a little relieved to hear he was to transfer to a newer prison camp. But New York would take him farther away from any hope of connecting with his brother in D.C. He didn't know that Alexander had been transferred to Fort Delaware.

Alexander left Washington June 15 and arrived at the Delaware prison camp June 17.[133] Col. Henry Burgwyn's brother, William H.S. Burgwyn, recounted the same route when he was transferred from Old Capitol Prison to Fort Delaware a few months later. The men rode the train from Washington through Baltimore. In Philadelphia, they marched from the depot to the wharf. The next day they rode about four hours in small tug boats to Fort Delaware, a marshy island with dikes and ditches built against the daily tidal floods. All their effects except clothing and one dollar were taken away and exchanged for sutler's tickets, including watches and canteens.

The men used the tidal ditches for wash water. Drinking water was brought in from a creek about ten miles away. Burgwyn, an officer, wrote that they had "bread and meat in the morning [and] bread meat and soup in the afternoon." He wrote to his mother, "It is much colder here than at Washington and our quarters more airy but withal as comfortable as could be expected. ... I continue in very good health and at this prison we have abundance of room for exercise though of the two prisons I would much prefer Washington City."[134]

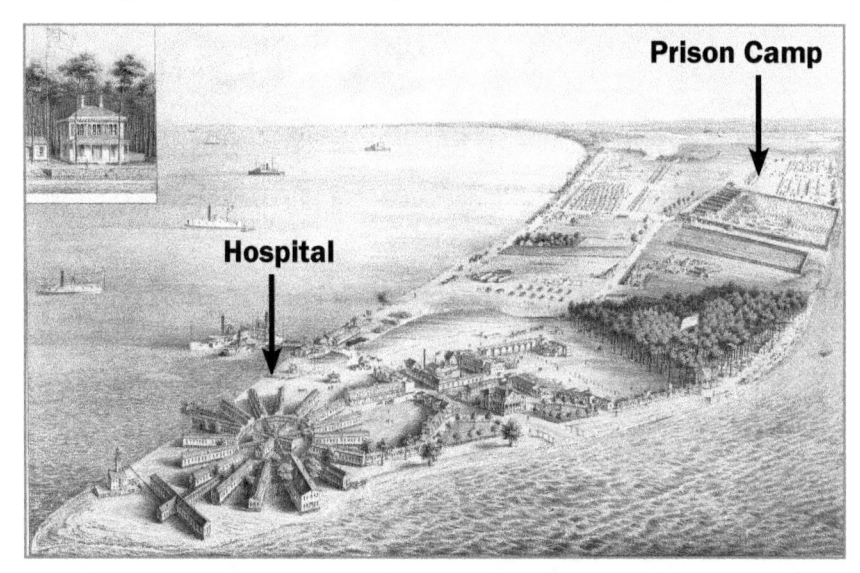

Point Lookout, Md., View of Hammond Gen'l Hospital & U.S. Gen'l Depot for Prisoners of War, 1864[135] *Notations added.*

As Alexander adjusted to prison life at Fort Delaware, Thomas was set to transfer from Point Lookout. About three days before his group was scheduled to leave, a terrible train wreck killed some of the prisoners in transit. The subsequent groups, including Thomas, travelled by ship.

Thomas had seen the bad treatment the guards subjected southerners to at Point Lookout. Rumors circulated about an unofficial order to let as many prisoners die as possible by neglect, rather than killing them on the battlefield. Did the prisoners wonder if a train wreck really happened? Had they simply shot or somehow killed those men so they'd have fewer of them to care for? Rumors and anxiety. If something happened to them on the way to New York, how would anybody who cared ever know the truth? If something happened to Thomas, would anybody back home ever know?

CHAPTER 16

SHADRACH

Petersburg, Virginia, 1864

Thomas' other brother, Shadrach, had missed the horrors of Gettysburg as well as many other smaller battles. He recovered from his illness and eventually returned to the Forty-Ninth Regiment. He was reported absent without leave starting December 28, 1863. He must have been excused; he received a uniform on March 20, indicating a return to duty sometime in the winter of 1864.[136]

The Forty-Ninth moved around eastern North Carolina with Gen. Matt Ransom's brigade. Their officers were planning to retake New Bern in May, when orders for reinforcements came from Gen. Lee in Virginia. Shadrach and the others marched to Kinston and took a train to Goldsboro, where "when we arrived there they had a long train ready for us with three engines, one at each end and one in the middle," wrote William A. Day, a private in Company I of the same regiment. "The whole Brigade, Branch's Battery, horses and all got aboard and pulled out for Petersburg, Virginia."[137]

A few miles short of Petersburg, they found the railroad destroyed: iron bent, ties burnt, and the bridge burned. The Yankees had been through just the day before. Shadrach and the others left the train and climbed up the banks. They formed ranks and marched the rest of the way.[138]

Arriving at Petersburg May 10, they were ordered farther north, as the opposing armies were already fighting uncomfortably close to Richmond. Ransom's brigade joined the fighting at Drewry's Bluff, a cliff on the west side of the James River, on May 13. The Federals were beginning to give way, when a line of them "which had extended around our right under cover of a piece of woods, opened a galling fire in our rear, and advanced to the charge from the woods on our right," wrote Lt. Thomas Roulhac of Company D. "Foot by foot [we] contested the ground until the charge in our front was broken, when the Forty-ninth and Twenty-fifth Regiments leaped over the works and poured a destructive volley into the ranks of the flanking party, before which their line melted away."[139] The regiment lost several men, including their quartermaster, and Gen. Ransom was wounded. The doctor and three litter-bearers were captured while tending the wounded.[140]

They spent the following days defending their position from Federal attacks. More men were lost in a successful charge on May 16, which allowed the Confederate army to freely move away to the Bermuda Hundred, a large area of land where the James and Appomattox rivers meet. The two armies played cat-and-mouse on both sides of the James River, until another brigade relieved them and they hurried back to defend Petersburg from Gen. Grant's approach.

"After marching all night of the 15th we reached Petersburg about 8 o'clock on the morning of the 16th, and were hurried to our fortifications on Avery's farm," Roulhac wrote.[141]

Virginia soldier George C. Eggleston writes an anecdotal account of the march into Petersburg in June, with the enemy firing at them, "the horses at a brisk trot, and the men on foot at a double quick. The enemy's battalions were already at the other end of Sycamore Street, and it was our task to drive them back before they should be reinforced."

The "good women of Petersburg ministered to us. They knew that we had been marching all night and that we were in a famishing condition. They knew also that we must not waste a moment if Petersburg, the key to Richmond, was not to be lost. So they formed themselves into platoons — God bless them! — Bearing gifts of sandwiches and coffee. We could not stop even to take, much less to eat, the food they offered, so they thrust their platoons between ours and marched backward as fast as we marched forward, serving their food and drink to us as we went. Every now and then a Federal shell would come bowling down the street, but these alert women. ... Not one of them showed the slightest fear."[142]

Shadrach's regiment continued marching towards Avery's farm, a railroad intersection southeast of the city. They arrived just in time to repulse a Federal attack. In the evening, they hurried north of town to help defend the Richmond turnpike. They continued up the turnpike, finally stopping to camp at midnight.

The next day, Shadrach got to ride the train back to Petersburg as they returned to Avery's farm. The following day, June 18, they held their part of the line "when the Federals charged our lines from one end to the other," wrote Day.[143] The soldiers were relieved by another brigade on June 19, perhaps retiring closer to the city for much-needed rest.[144]

The people who lived in Petersburg continued to live their lives as best they could during the long siege and tried to encourage the soldiers; some women even came to the lines one day to sing. Eggleston wrote, "During all those weary months the good women of Petersburg went about their household affairs with fifteen-inch shells dropping occasionally into their boudoirs or uncomfortably near to their kitchen ranges. Yet they paid no attention to any danger that threatened themselves."[145]

The townspeople also helped make gunpowder. "All the window-weights in all the houses, and all the other leaden things that could be melted down, were converted into bullets." Eggleston implies that the support of the residents fueled the Confederates' "stubborn resistance."[146]

The Forty-Ninth returned to the lines June 21. They dug trenches with picks and shovels and wheelbarrows, deep enough so they could walk from place to place and stay out of the line of fire. Although they worked primarily at night, sharpshooters with rifles plagued them.[147] One of those bullets hit Shadrach.

*Blandford Church, Petersburg, Va., April 1865, by
Timothy H. O'Sullivan*[148]

His records say "killed in battle," which might simply refer to the long siege of Petersburg.[149] After being cut off from news in Virginia for several days, the Raleigh *Daily Confederate* reported about larger battles on the other days, and, "There was brisk skirmishing throughout Thursday, but no general engagement."[150] Another division used local knowledge of ravines to defend the Weldon railroad around that time, but if Shadrach was with the Forty-Ninth on the east side of Petersburg, he was probably hit by sniper fire.

T. W. Dandridge, assistant surgeon to the Forty-Ninth, reported Shadrach in a list of men killed and wounded from 21 June to 1 July. "This list shows how severe the sharpshooting is," he wrote. "Our men though are satisfied that they hold a [fair] hand against the enemy at this game."[151] Dispatches to other newspapers (which finally reached them in July) reported Shadrach's death on Tuesday, June 21.[152] The 17-year-old North Carolinian was buried in an unmarked grave near Blandford Church, a run-down eighteenth-century brick church with a Revolutionary-era cemetery.[153]

CHAPTER 17
ELMIRA PRISON CAMP

Elmira, New York, July 1864

THE BOAT MIGHT HAVE SEEMED SAFER after the train accident, but Thomas and the other prisoners were packed into its belly like cattle. Walter Addison, who was also transferred from Point Lookout, Maryland to Elmira, New York, wrote, "About twelve hundred men were crowded upon this old tub between decks with only the hatches open, and there they remained crowded together like sheep for many days. ... The condition and sufferings of the prisoners [in the holds] was indeed horrible, and a large number of the men being already sick when placed on board their wretched condition upon the voyage can be imagined better than described. ... Think of their journey by sea, several hundred miles, crowded together as we were, with so many sick in the sweltering heat of July. It was on a par with the condition of the Yankee slave ships with a cargo of human souls purchased with a cargo of Boston rum." Some died on the way.[154]

Thomas arrived in New York July 30. He marched with the other prisoners to Elmira and entered the former small fort that had been expanded by a large stockade to surround the prison camp. Low mountains surrounded the camp, with the old city of Elmira to the north and east and the Chemung River to the south. The men marched down a wide street between the stockade and the city and into the main entrance. The view was heart-sinkingly familiar: acres of white tents — more than a thousand of them, intended to house four men each.[155]

Buildings to the right were the kitchens, hospital, and officers' quarters. To the south stood a long mess hall and an overflow branch of the river that ran through canals under the fence, Foster's Pond.[156] Guards patrolled on a walkway built into the outside of the tall stockade. This place also had a dead line; they lit globe lamps every night so they could see any prisoner who approached the fence.[157]

Confederate prisoners arrived by the hundreds from other Union camps. In the fall, Elmira had over nine thousand prisoners — more than twice its intended capacity. Barracks were gradually being built, but about half the men still slept in tents.[158] A couple of enterprising locals built towers just outside the camp, charging visitors ten to fifteen cents to climb up and watch the teeming beehive of captured Rebels. By late September, however, the camp commander had the towers removed on the suspicion that spies might use them to communicate with prisoners.[159]

Thomas and the other prisoners adjusted to camp life without knowing how long they would stay. Rumors almost daily fed their

Elmira camp for Confederate prisoners with tents, by Moulton & Larkin (1864)[160]

hopes of being exchanged. They lined up for mandatory roll call every morning, regardless of weather or individual illnesses. They ate standing up in the mess hall twice a day: four ounces of bread or some crackers and a small piece of salt pork or pickled beef in the morning, another piece of bread and salty broth in the evening. The meager rations left them feeling a constant, "sharp hunger."[161]

The lack of any fruit or vegetables led to an outbreak of scurvy, which brought skin sores and sore, fragile mouths. Malnutrition drained the men of energy and resistance to diseases. Although the camp surgeon requested a better diet for the prisoners, Secretary of War Edwin Stanton had already cut rations twice in a policy of retaliation against the South, after emaciated Union prisoners had been returned, their descriptions splashed across Northern newspapers. With the backing of senators and congressmen but without the official approval of President Lincoln, Stanton used bureaucratic rules and delays to prevent any relief from getting to the prisoners, even when compassionate Northerners tried to help.[162]

Michael J. Haley's brother was one of the guards. Haley wrote, "It was so distasteful to him that after a few months he applied to get back to his regiment. This was during the 'retaliatory' period, when Stanton was mowing a wide swath." Their mother cried when he told them how the prisoners suffered.[163]

In an effort to survive, the scrappy soldiers developed a thriving black market. They weren't allowed to have money — it was kept on account at the commissary — so tobacco became the standard exchange. The men used their ample time to create trinkets, such as bone carvings, rings and buttons, and some of the camp officers sold them in town. Any kind of food would be sold or traded, from apples to rats. Large rats overran the camp, especially in the refuse by the cook house. An officer's dog wouldn't last long. Haley wrote, "My brother said that a cat, notwithstanding its proverbial nine lives, wouldn't live five minutes in the Rebel prison at Elmira." Any man caught eating a dog or rat or selling such on the black market would either be hung by the thumbs or forced to wear a wooden barrel all day, the "barrel shirt."[164]

Diseases added to misery and mortality. Groups of transferred prisoners brought smallpox into the camp. The ever-present dysentery, with its accompanying diarrhea, was no excuse for missing roll call. Lice were prevalent. The only place to wash up — or not — was Foster's Pond, which became a sewer. Fellow prisoner Walter Addison witnessed the surgeon-in-chief prescribe arsenic for forty-five patients, all of whom died shortly thereafter.[165]

In mid-October 1864, about 2,000 sick and wounded were finally exchanged.[166] The snow started in November. An unusually cold winter with subfreezing temperatures descended on Elmira. The Southerners only had lightweight, ragged clothing. Those without coats wore their thin blankets around during the day. Frostbite attacked feet and other body parts. Several men died from the resulting gangrene. Work projects stalled because the ground was frozen. Foster's Pond froze over.[167]

Thomas eventually lived in one of the barracks, which were finished by Christmas. Each building slept 112 men in three levels of bunks. They slept two men to a six-by-four-foot bunk, head-to-foot. There was no bedding to soften the boards. The buildings were made of rough planks set on blocks, which made them very drafty. A single stove stood in the middle of each long building.[168]

Roll Call, showing Elmira prison camp with finished barracks in 1865 (Reproduced by permission of Chemung County Historical Society, Elmira, NY)

Virginian John Opie wrote, "Imagine, if you can, with the weather ten or fifteen degrees below zero, one hundred men trying to keep warm by one stove. Each morning the men crawled out of their bunks shivering and half frozen, when a scuffle, and frequently a fight, for a place by the fire occurred."[169]

News of various battles brought mixed feelings; although the prisoners wanted the South to win, reports of Rebel losses came with hope for the end of the war and freedom to return home. About half of the men applied to take the Oath of Allegiance.[170] Thomas was one of them, applying on December 16. He omitted his first year of service, saying that he had volunteered in 1862 to avoid conscription.[171]

The days around Christmas were mild, but melting ice left the camp muddy and slippery. South Carolina soldier Wilbur Gramling wrote that Christmas seemed like any other day. The next day he wrote, "It is reported that Savannah has fallen with 20,000 prisoners. Quite sickly in camp again, from 15 to 25 die a day. Small pox is growing worse every day."[172]

Amidst the bitter cold, hunger and threat of smallpox, some of the prisoners tried to find a little fun where they could. North Carolinian Lewis Leon wrote about dancing in their quarters. "Some of the men put a white handkerchief around one of their arms, and these act as the ladies. We have a jolly good time."[173]

Heavy snow fell before the end of the year and the blustery cold returned. About four feet of snow lingered through the early months of 1865.[174] Taking the oath of allegiance or not didn't seem to matter much, as men continued to wait for an exchange. Finally, in February, groups of men by state, with large groups of the sick, began to be sent out on parole. North Carolina and Virginia were to be last. Gramling complained that a bribe got a man's name on the list. He wrote in his diary that deaths were increasing, "from 20 to 30 every day out of about 7000 men."[175]

Richard Dibrell, who received exchanged prisoners in Georgia in March, noted their deplorable condition. "They were so enfeebled and emaciated that we lifted them like little children. Many of them were like living skeletons. Indeed, there was one poor boy about 17 years old. ... He was nothing but skin and bone, besides this, he was literally eaten up by vermin. He died in the hospital in a few days."[176] The boy was about two years older than Thomas.

The snow and ice finally melted, causing the Chemung River to overflow on March 16. A group of camp officers and prisoners worked to evacuate the hospital, moving more than two hundred patients to old barracks on high ground. The water kept rising, flooding the rest of the camp by the next day. The men climbed up as the water rose up to six feet deep at the barracks, depending on location, drowning the lower bunks. "We were confined in the higher bunks for a day or two with nothing to eat or drink but the dirty river water," said Virginian prisoner John R. King. Men in row boats brought them a little food. Then the water receded enough so they could wade through camp and reach the water pump for drinking water.[177]

They had been confined because most of the stockade had washed away. The men worked on repairs to the damaged cookhouse and other parts of the camp. Word of Lee's surrender came in April, bringing hope for the end of the war.[178] The miseries of Elmira led to one of the highest death rates of all the prison camps, at 24 percent.[179] The survivors waited, amid more news of surrenders and negotiations. As the weeks passed, a few hundred at the time were called to roll and shipped out.

Thomas' name was finally called. He was measured and described, then he made his mark on the roll. Approximately fifteen years old, he was six feet, one and a half inches tall. On May 29, he likely stood in a group of two or three hundred prisoners, raised his right hand, and swore allegiance to the United States. Thomas was officially freed at the Elmira Depot.[180]

The government provided transportation to the freed prisoners, as well as a sparse two days' rations and a parole paper. Those who had money on account could hurry to the sutler's office to claim it, so they could buy something to eat on the long trip home. Walter Addison described being "crowded into cattle cars" at Elmira, then loaded into the cargo hold of a steamboat to reach Richmond.[181] Thomas wanted to travel to Washington, D.C., not realizing that Alexander had been transferred to Delaware.[182] Not finding his brother, he probably continued his journey to North Carolina. After four long, miserable years in the army, Thomas was going home.

Thomas Maness' Prisoner of War cards, 11-12[183]

CHAPTER 18
MOVING HOME

Southern Maryland, 2003

I HAD HAD ENOUGH OF THE military. Since about 2000, the Department of Defense had tried to cut its famously high costs by meshing defense contractors, civil servants and military personnel into "Integrated Test Teams." While more efficient in theory, each group insisted on its own supervisors, which left me in lower middle management with as many bosses as workers. Like mini-politicians, each supervisor wanted to cut costs after already cutting costs, preside over redundant daily meetings, and refused to sign off on reports that shed less than stellar light on their company or product.

Add some bipolar personalities to that mix, and this quiet southern girl had more than she could stand. I stayed late to get my work finished after the "bosses" left, then I went home in tears. By early 2003, I had chest pains. My father had died of a heart attack at the age of 39 — only a few years older than I was. Something had to change. I quietly trained my replacement, took a month-long vacation to Australia and, after returning, turned in my notice.

My whole career, including summer internships during college, had played out in the security and benefits of government service. I had no idea what I was going to do.

I researched and daydreamed about wild-hair jobs, from joining the Peace Corps to teaching at a private school on the Zuni reservation in New Mexico. However, the fact that my mom had been diagnosed with cancer about a year ago tugged at me. She was doing well, now, but I needed to move closer to home, not farther away. So, I applied for teaching positions in North Carolina. I hadn't made my decision early enough to catch the summer hiring for the fall semester, but I scanned the online openings and applied for jobs that opened up during the school year. Certainly I could teach — as an engineer I'd taken years of math classes, continuing into graduate school. I had been a volunteer tutor and chaperoned youth events at my church.

After another interview that didn't work out, I had a successful interview with Chatham County schools. They offered me a position teaching math at Northwood High School. There was one catch, though. A certain number of days of mandatory training was required before I could teach in January, and we were running up against the winter break. Could I start in two weeks?

I had a house, pets, furniture, fourteen years worth of clutter that I could never seem to handle because of the late working hours, and no place to live when I got there. You bet I can start in two weeks!

✯ ✯ ✯

I FELL INTO THE FRANTIC DAILY life of a new high school teacher in Pittsboro, North Carolina. My great-aunt, Mary Maness Payseur, lived nearby. With her help, I found a little old house in Siler City for rent, with glass doorknobs and a persnickety gas heater mounted in the living-room wall. The 17-mile commute to work was pleasant, via the new bypass through old farms and scenic country-

Aunt Mary (Mary Maness Payseur) with the author in Pittsboro, 2005

side. Sometimes Aunt Mary and I met for lunch at one of the restaurants near the old Pittsboro courthouse, a landmark in the center of a roundabout with roads that branched away in four directions.

I had put Thomas Maness aside. Other branches of my family were easier, especially the Quakers. A distant cousin had written a book about the English family, with names and dates back to the 1600s. But Thomas was just too hard. I'd looked for George and Mary Maness on the census records in North Carolina and in Arkansas. Those seemed like common names and I expected to find plenty of wrong families. Surprisingly, I didn't find any George and Mary together. I had looked for Mary only, as a possible widow with a child named Thomas — no luck with that, either.

A few years earlier, in May 2001, Momma, Oscar and I had teamed up again to attend a Maness family reunion in Moore County. It was a nice potluck deal, outdoors by the old Maness family cemetery, a small collection of graves that dated back to the early 1800s. I didn't even bother to take pictures. The names on the graves were unfamiliar and I still wasn't sure we were even connected to this family.

Thurman Maness was there. He and others shared stories of Shadrach, Meshach, and Abednego, their Scottish ancestors. I copied Thomas S. Maness' Civil War military record from a lady named Mary Hensen, not realizing I would see it many times later in libraries. A large man on the bench near Thurman introduced himself as Don McCaskill. He was writing a book, and wanted to know all about our family. He wrote down everything I said, which made me nervous. Why would a real genealogist write down everything and never ask for a source? Plus, although identity theft hadn't hit anyone I knew, yet, my work with the Department of Defense made me wary of giving out personal information. So we told him Papaw and Paw's names, but refused to give him our birthdates.

"If you ever find anything else, please let me know," he said, scribbling down his contact information. He ripped a page off of a small yellow ledger pad and handed it to me.

That note lay jammed and forgotten in the many boxes I didn't have time to unpack in Siler City. Although I'd enjoyed tutoring, I simply wasn't made to stand in front of a high school classroom and maintain tight control of twenty-plus other human beings. I neglected the good students, distracted by the constant battle of wills with other students who didn't want to be there. I worked long hours, again, and caught so many voracious colds I couldn't visit my mother when she was in the hospital. Once again, I gave months of notice, refusing to desert my students in the middle of the semester, and quit at the end of 2004.

CHAPTER 19
HOME
Moore County, 1865

Thomas and Alexander made their ways back to North Carolina. Released May 3, 1865, Alexander's trip may have been similar to William Burgwyn's. Burgwyn left Fort Delaware in a steamer on February 27. "We were all put 400 privates and 200 officers in the between decks in bunks so close together you could not sit up and sentinels put on the hatchways and we were compelled to stay in there." They landed near City Point and marched to Richmond. Burgwyn travelled several days by train through Danville, Virginia to Greensboro, North Carolina, then on to Raleigh.[184]

Shadrach never returned. The siege of Petersburg had lasted more than nine grueling months. Over 30,000 soldiers were added to his unmarked grave at Blandford Church cemetery.[185]

Thomas' brother wasn't the only Maness to die at Petersburg. Their cousin, Rev. Reuben Maness, had joined the "Randolph Rangers," Company G of the Forty-Sixth Regiment. He was preaching to the troops in early August when a sniper's bullet pierced his neck. He died a day or two later. His brothers were Isaac, who had deserted from the Twenty-Sixth Regiment, and Thomas P. Maness, who had fought the home guard and rescued conscriptees in Carthage. Although "Tommy"

Blandford Church Cemetery in 2017, looking toward the section where more than 30,000 men were buried during the Civil War

had avoided the army altogether, he'd promised Reuben that, if the worst should happen, he would bring his body home.

Reuben must have told his friends about the promise. They buried him in an ammunition box and marked the grave with a wooden cross, then sent word to his family. True to his promise, in the fall of 1865, Tommy took a covered wagon and made the long journey to Petersburg. He found the grave and retrieved his brother's remains. The round-trip by horse and wagon took about a month. Every night, Tommy would tell his silent passenger, "We're a little closer to home." Reuben was buried in the cemetery at Pleasant Hill Methodist Church in Moore County.[186] Two generations later Tommy's grandson, Thurman Maness, placed a marker for Shadrach next to Reuben's grave.[187]

Thomas and Alexander must have had plenty to catch up on, perhaps comparing prison camps; perhaps avoiding or only alluding to battlefield horrors. Both of the dark-haired boys had grown tall; Thomas now had an inch over his older brother. Their three sisters were living with different families on farms in Bensalem township, Moore County, by 1870, so that might have been where the brothers found them in late 1865. Leanda Cain lived with John and Mary Dowd in Curriesville, Bensalem township.[188] Mary Catherine might have still been with Ira's family in Prosperity, where she'd lived with Alexander as a child. By 1870, she was living with John and Julia Bailey and their two young children in Carter's Mills.[189]

Reuben Maness' (left) and Shadrach Maness' (right) tombstones at Pleasant Hill United Methodist Cemetery in Moore County, N.C. in 2015

Lundy Jane, the oldest, lived with John and Margaret Buie in Curriesville.[190] Lundy Jane had an affair with "Dumps" Stutts (possibly Dempsey Stutts of Gold Region) and became pregnant after the war was over. Hugh Alexander Maness was born June 1, 1866.[191]

Thomas moved to Chatham County, probably looking for work in the devastated Reconstruction South. He met Mary Craton, a blacksmith's daughter who lived in Pittsboro. Thomas had probably heard his fellow soldiers talk fondly of their wives and sweethearts back home. He might have survived that horrible year in the prison camp dreaming about the life he'd make for himself, with the kind of family he'd never had. He married Mary on September 5, 1866.[192]

Thomas had been pretending to be older than he was for so long, it had become part of his identity. He probably had to lie about his age in order to marry; he was barely 16. His bride was nearly a decade older. A veteran whose life had been in danger many times wouldn't have wanted to ask permission for anything — even if he had parents. Although their marriage record does not include ages, in the 1870 census Thomas was listed as 25 years old, when he was really about 20.[193]

Thomas and Mary settled down in Pittsboro, where he worked as a farm hand. They had their firstborn son, William Nuton Maness, in September 1867. James Robert came along two years later in October

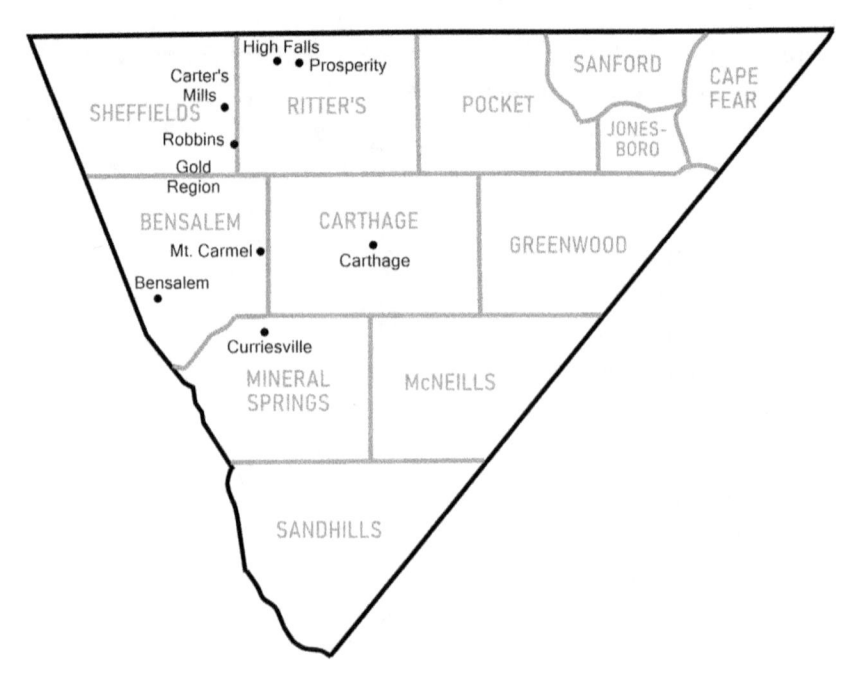

Simplified Map of Moore County, showing townships and places where Thomas Maness' family lived[194]

1869. William was Mary's brother's name and Robert was her father's name. In 1871, a little girl joined the family. They named her Martha, which was Mary's mother's name.[195] They were blessed.

Nobody knows what happened after that — whether Thomas got the "seven-year itch," or experienced what we now call post-traumatic stress disorder, or if he simply couldn't provide for his family as a farmer. But one day, Thomas left.

CHAPTER 20
BACK TO THE MYSTERY

Randolph County, North Carolina, 2005

In the spring of 2005 I took online classes in case I wanted to try different kinds of teaching. I also took an online writing course. I had savings, and planned to find something by the end of the year. With my education, surely I could find a job, even if it was a lot lower pay. Still not knowing what I wanted to do, I put my Maryland house up for sale and bought a condo in my hometown in Randolph County.

I spent the rest of the year finishing and publishing a genealogy book about my hometown church and spending time with my mom. A widow for decades, she went out to dinner most weeks with her single brother, who lived in my grandparents' house on the next road. After Momma passed away in October 2005, I tried to spend time with my uncle. We would go to one of the local diners and chat about everything over fried comfort food. He would ask if I had found anything more on the Manesses.

"No, I haven't done much on that side."

"That man that kept asking questions at the reunion, d'ja ever hear from him?" Oscar asked.

"No." I shook my head. I couldn't even remember his name, but figured I had it scribbled on a scrap of paper somewhere. As far as I was concerned, the man was a gatherer, not a serious genealogist. Like the people I'd met at genealogy events who bragged about the number of names in their databases, but never bothered to cite their sources.

Oscar said, "I think he was just hunting for information, and we're not going to hear from him."

I didn't think he could help us, anyway. "He's just writing his book," I said.

Oscar finished up his greens. "I want to go talk to Thurman Maness, again, and see what we can find out."

I chewed and tried to choose my words. "Do you think he's still around?"

"I don't know. I guess he'd be getting on up in years, wouldn't he?"

Every time, we'd agree that we shouldn't put it off, but our busy schedules got in the way. Oscar drove trucks all over the country. I had taken a part-time job writing for the local newspaper, and our schedules for a day trip rarely met. I spent more time working on the English family. My sister, her husband, and I took our dream trip to England, Ireland and Scotland in 2006, where I researched that Quaker branch back to the seventeenth century.

Around 2008, I finally told my uncle, "We'd better not put it off any longer or we're going to miss him. What are you doing this weekend?" Oscar agreed that we'd better check as to Thurman's health and whereabouts. He called Lacy Garner, the man who'd put him in touch with Thurman when we visited years ago. It was a good thing we checked. Thurman's wife had passed away and he'd moved to a nursing home in Southern Pines, about a half hour farther away than Carthage.

Our schedules clashed again as Oscar delivered trucks around the country. But opportunity came my way; in March, my newspaper assigned me to cover a story in Pinehurst, not far from Southern Pines. I called the nursing home, verified that Thurman still lived there, and arranged a side trip.

CHAPTER 21

PANDORA

Near the Guilford and Randolph County line, 1874

Thomas probably worked his way from place to place, chopping timber and hiring himself out as manual labor. He worked his way up to lower Guilford County and met a young, doe-eyed girl, Sarah Pandora Wall. According to later pictures, Pandora wore her dark hair pulled back in a bun, with a part in the middle. Her father, Jimmie Wall, had been a struggling farmer who might have died before the war. Pandora lived with her mother and stepfather, Martha and Gilbert Chappell, and four siblings, including a brand new baby sister. They probably lived in the Centre community near the Deep River, on land that had been passed down through the Gossett family to her mother.[196]

In 1870, Pandora and her stepbrother Jonathan were in school. Centre Friends Meeting, with financial help from Baltimore Friends after the war, had conducted at least five schools in the community. Less than half the children were Quakers, and most paid one dollar per month for three to four months of school. Pandora may have attended the school at Centre Friends or at Providence, which were partially supported through donations.[197] So she learned to read and write.

Thomas married Pandora on June 25, 1874, at the local justice of the peace's house. She was 14. Perhaps her mother was eager to find

Pandora the security of her own home, or to have one less mouth to feed. She not only signed her permission on the marriage license, she also stretched Pandora's age to 16.

Thomas no longer had to lie about his age, twenty-five. He gave his parents' names as George and Mary and let the clerk or justice assume their surnames, a "little white lie." The bigger lie was an important omission to both the justice and his new family — the fact that he was already married.[198]

Within a year, Pandora was expecting their first child. Still in rural North Carolina, Thomas' new home wasn't any easier than the places he'd left. Some families, including Pandora's older brother, Jonathan Wiley Wall, had moved to the midwestern states for rich land and new beginnings. Some men travelled wherever the expansion of railroads and mining offered opportunities. Thomas told his new family he was going to look for work at the Bertha Zinc Mine in Virginia. He drove off with a buckboard wagon and some blankets.[199]

Pandora gave birth to a son on July 8, 1875, Franklin Wiley Maness. She probably named him for her brother, known to later generations as "Uncle Wiley." He, in turn, may have been named for their uncle and former neighbor, Norwood Wiley, who had also moved out west.[200] Pandora's mother and stepfather ended up with another mouth to feed, after all. Frankie and his youngest aunt, Mary Jane Chappell, were just a year and a half apart. They would have grown up together like brother and sister. Time passed and Frankie grew, as they waited for his father to return. He never did.[201]

Frank Wiley Maness with an unidentified young woman (possibly his youngest aunt, Mary Jane Chappell), ca. 1895[202]

CHAPTER 22

NANCY

Pulaski County, Virginia, 1875-1876

Thomas Maness might have found a job in the Bertha Zinc Mine in Pulaski County, Virginia. L. C. Vass, a traveler from North Carolina, described this booming area in 1890. He described the town of Pulaski as an "eight year old town … 1,900 feet above the sea." He visited the luxurious Maple Shade Hotel, and he commented on the churches that had sprung up in recent years. "Extensive zinc works are located here. It was interesting to follow the process of taking the crude ore — just so much dirt — roasting it, grinding it, and then heating it terribly, as the colored flames licked out their variegated tongues, from hundreds of retorts, and finally receiving the silvery masses for commerce. Nine furnaces are turning out 1,630 pounds each every 24 hours. I saw the masses of shining blocks piled up for the world."

Vass comments on an iron furnace: "In the opposite quarter of the village are these mills. How they did roar…. So many times a day this process goes on, and the world's machinery is kept active. The ores for both iron and zinc are brought from a distance of 10 or 15 miles.

"Can it be wondered that Pulaski is growing and land agents are active? '1,000 acres in lots for sale.' Such advertisements flare at you on every band. A splendid brick Presbyterian church is nearing completion there. It will cost $8,000. ... Fine edifices are dotting hills and valleys on every side here."[203]

Somehow Thomas met a young woman named Nancy Pool. A middle child of eight children, she came from a farming family, though later generations would be connected with the railroad and the mines. Only the oldest boy, Charles, learned to read and write. Nancy and her parents, Moses and Matilda Pool, lived in Giles County, nestled between Pulaski County and the modern West Virginia.[204]

Whether or not Thomas found a job at the mine, he was calling himself a farmer by the time he married Nancy on December 13, 1876. He gave his parents' names as George and Polly. He said he was 26 years old, born in Wake County, North Carolina. He also said he was single.[205]

The young couple had a daughter, Fannie Betty Maness, in October of 1877. Nancy's father, Moses, died that December. We don't know how long Thomas stayed in Virginia. Nancy was living with her mother and siblings in the 1880 census. Curiously, she was listed as single, with no mention of little Fannie.[206]

Opportunities were good for a hard worker, if he could get away from the farm. In 1891 the *Economist-Falcon* reported, "The pay-roll of the Bertha Zinc Works at Pulaski City, Va., now exceeds $26,000 monthly, and their capacity is to be largely increased."[207] With such promising sources of income, who knows when and why Thomas left Virginia. He was not the only working man from North Carolina. In 1892, North Carolina's Lexington *Dispatch* reported, "Several miners who have been working at Bertha Zinc mines returned last week."[208] Thomas probably left Virginia to either look for work, or for a job that took him out of the area. This time, however, he might not have left for good.

CHAPTER 23
ORAL HISTORY

Southern Pines, Moore County, March 7, 2008

THE NURSE GUIDED ME TO THURMAN Maness' room. I felt a pang as she told me how he was looking forward to my visit. I'm a total stranger, I thought. I hoped he had some family to visit him. "We just love him!" the nurse whispered in the hall. She added that I would have to speak up, so he could hear me.

Thurman sat in a chair by the bed. I'd forgotten the large features, but immediately recognized him. One of those studio portraits, probably taken for the church directory, of him and his late wife Verdia hung on the wall behind him. I greeted him and he asked me to pull my chair up close. Closer. Although I wasn't used to having a non-family member only a couple of inches from my face, I realized that his blindness wasn't complete, and he wanted to see me as well as he could. I soon felt at ease despite the closeness. He was almost a hundred years old, after all.

I asked his permission to use my tape recorder, then had to ask again, louder. I had access to a tiny, high-tech digital recorder that my editor had allowed me to use for this as well as the story I had just covered in Pinehurst. Thurman said that was fine. I asked him about Thomas Swain Maness, his relative who might be our Thomas Maness, and the stories started to flow.

Thurman's grandfather, Presley Maness, was Swain's first cousin, and Thurman's father had remembered him.[209] "Before the Civil War, they said Swain was a fine boy. Just a fine boy. But when he come back, he's a different boy," Thurman said. "He come back just as mean as a snake." Swain went to South Carolina, looking for a job at a sawmill. When he got there, the foreman said they didn't have any jobs open. Swain decided to stick around for a few days. The next morning, he went back. "One colored fellow didn't show up," Thurman said. "Swain got a job. Later on, a week or two, they found the fellow over there in the woods covered up with brush, dead." Swain never came right out and admitted to killing the man, but his friends in Moore County figured he was the one that did it.[210]

Thurman's father said Swain was smart. I recognized the regional dialect, where "smart" means "hard-working." Thurman said, "He didn't bother anybody unless they bothered him. Well, one time down, somewhere, I believe he said down in Georgia, something happened. Somebody said, 'If I meet up with that Swain Maness, again, I'll kill him.' Swain met up with him. They got in a fight. He said he killed him." He got out of that because witnesses said the man had threatened to kill him.

Thurman interrupted himself. "A woman from Randolph County asked me about him a few years ago. What was her name?"

Old Moore County Courthouse[211]

"I'll bet that was me."

"What's that?"

I raised my voice. "That was me! I'm the woman from Randolph County."

"Oh! I remember you. But I didn't remember your name." He launched into another story. Swain had a job working for a man when the sheriff came to arrest him. "My daddy ... said the sheriff went after him and read the warrant to him. He said I have to take you in to Carthage, put you in jail. Said Swain told him, 'I'm not going to jail.'" The sheriff insisted. Swain said, "Listen, Sheriff, if you try to take me, one of us won't be leaving here, and it ain't gonna be me."

"My daddy said Swain had his hand on his pistol in his hip pocket. Said if he even see the sheriff start for his gun, he aimed to shoot him. Said the sheriff finally said, well you come down there tomorrow, at 10 o'clock. Swain said, 'Yes, I'll come down there at 10 o'clock for you to try me.'" Swain showed up at the courthouse at 10 o'clock. He was acquitted of the charges. He walked out of the courtroom and down the courthouse steps, shooting in the air five times. He'd had his pistol the whole time, and nobody tried to take it from him! Thurman said, "Nobody come out there and bother him. Swain said, 'I woke up that ol' judge!'"[212]

We had a pleasant visit, and I remembered to ask him a little about his own family as well as ancestors. He had a son in Georgia. The nurse's words came back to me, about how he'd looked forward to my visit. I asked him about the DNA test that had been mentioned in phone conversations. I didn't know much about this new trend in genealogy, but I had been wondering if we could compare our family to his, since his father was Swain's first cousin.

He answered, "Lacy Garner, the pharmacist at Carthage, he's the man that does a lot of that work." Thurman had provided the cells from inside his cheek, but he didn't know anything about the process or what company they had used. As I stood up to leave, he took my hand and said, "Come back and visit me again. Please do."

"I will." What else could I say? As I walked down the hall I wondered if I could keep my word. We lived hours apart, and he was nearly 100 years old.

CHAPTER 24
TRAVELING MAN
1880-1895

THE INCRIMINATING STORIES ABOUT THOMAS MANESS must have come from his own mouth, tall tales among his kinsmen in Moore County. No record has been found that puts him in South Carolina; however, he lived for a while in Anson County, North Carolina, which borders South Carolina.

White Store township, right on the state line, had been a thriving plantation community before the war. In March 1865, Gen. Judson Kilpatrick's cavalry, as part of Sherman's army, burned houses, stole valuables and destroyed food stores throughout the area. Louisa Kelly, a small child at the time, grew up in the area as people struggled to rebuild, nostalgic for antebellum days.[213]

Louisa never knew her father, Martin Kelly, if he was the same Martin Kelly who enlisted in the Confederate Army February 24, 1862. Louisa was born the following December. A former brickmason, Martin was wounded in the right leg at Drewry's Bluff on May 16, 1864 (where Shadrach Maness was also fighting). His leg had to be amputated. He died in the hospital in Richmond on May 22, 1864.[214] Louisa's mother, Louiza (or Louisa) Kelly, also appears to have died young.[215]

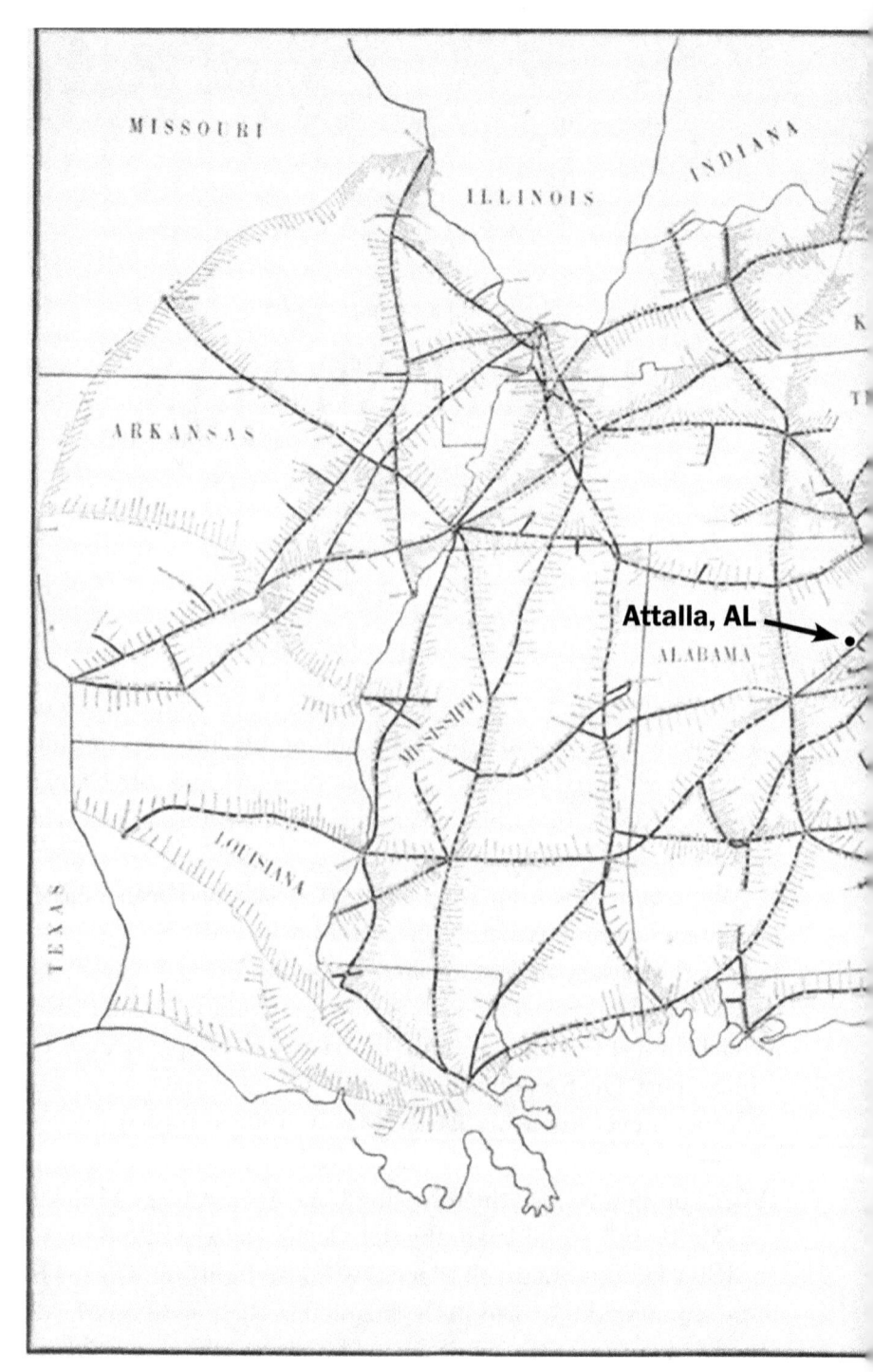

Map of the Southern Express Company, 1884[216]

Dublin, VA

Wadesboro, NC

FOR SALE BY
WALKER, EVANS & COGSWELL.
CHARLESTON, S. C.

MAP
OF THE
SOUTHERN EXPRESS COMPANY
COMPILED BY
A. M. RICHARDSON.
Charleston, S. C.

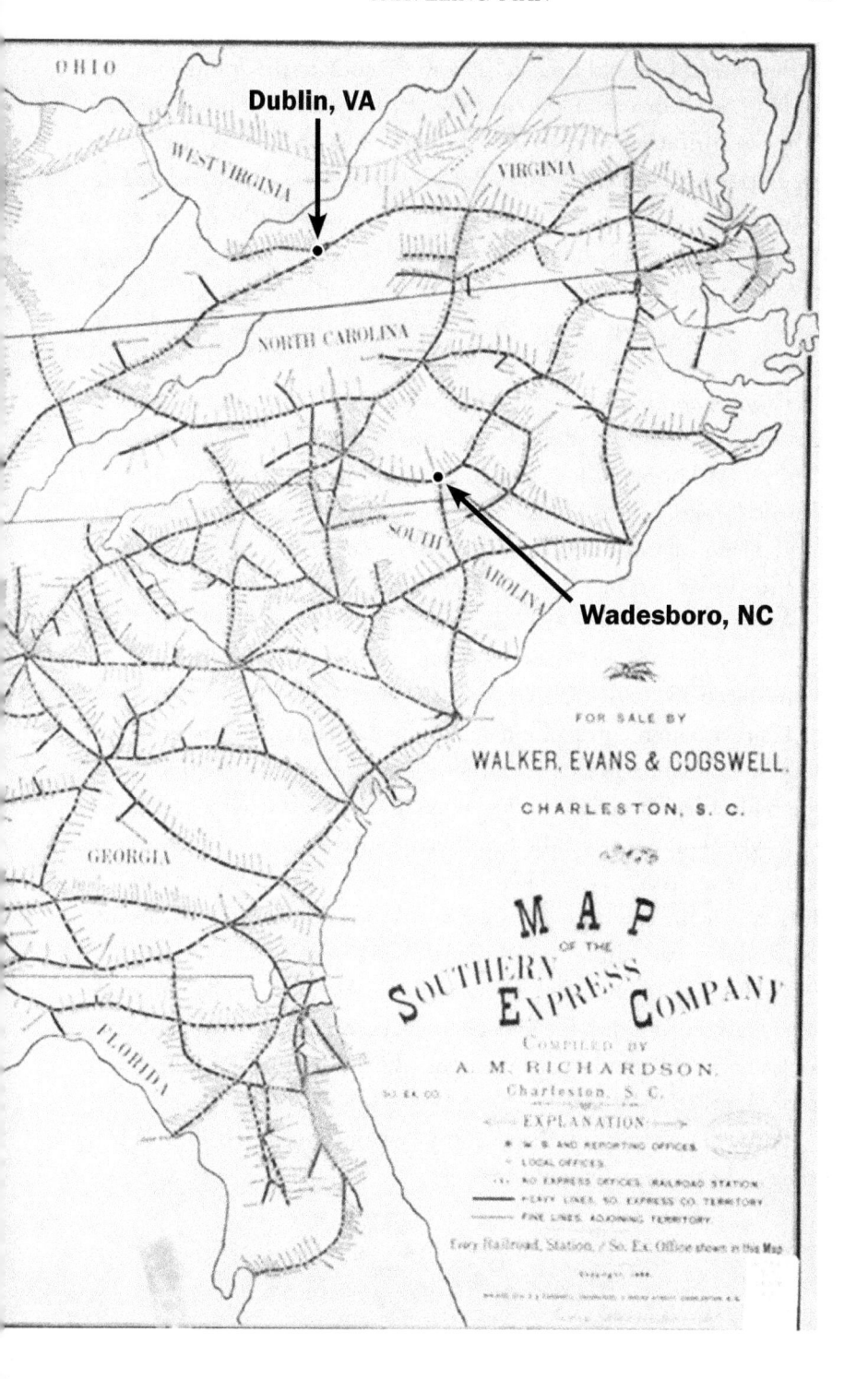

Seventeen-year-old Louisa Kelly was a cook in the Johnson household in Lanesboro township in June 1880, possibly living next door to her grandfather and sister. Thomas Maness married Louisa on December 12, 1880, four days before her eighteenth birthday. They were married by a Baptist minister in James Treadway's house in White Store, possibly her uncle's or cousin's home. In a bout of sloppy recording, the marriage license states that none of their parents' names were known, except that Louisa's mother, also Louisa Kelly, was dead.[217]

Thomas and Louisa might have had children that didn't survive.[218] Around August of 1885, Thomas was back in Virginia. His wife, Nancy, had Thomas Cleveland Maness in May 1886.[219] But Thomas returned, regularly, to Louisa in Anson County, North Carolina. They had Herman Fantom on June 5, 1886 — only one month younger than his unknown brother in Virginia![220]

A few years later, on April 29, 1888, Thomas married Willie Stewart in Etowah County, Alabama. Their daughter, Cora Elizabeth, was born March 13, 1889.[221]

There are no records of nineteenth-century railroad workers, much less itinerant laborers that rode the rails to find jobs, so we don't know which lifestyle Thomas led. Plus, most of the 1890 federal census was destroyed. But a map of the Southern Express Railroad shows stops or depots at Attalla and Gadsden, Alabama, where Willie lived, and Dublin, Virginia, where Nancy lived. Wadesboro, North Carolina, near Louisa, was a hub connecting three railroads.[222]

Thomas probably never returned to his Alabama family and might never have seen Cora. He was back in Anson County by late 1890; Louisa had William Harvey on August 22, 1891. She had John Franklin on April 19, 1892.[223]

Thomas was back in Moore County sometime in 1895. His trips home to Louisa finally ended.[224]

CHAPTER 25

LACY GARNER AND THURMAN MANESS

Moore County, July 24, 2010

I DON'T REMEMBER EXACTLY WHEN UNCLE Oscar went into the hospital with cancer. I didn't know he had also had leukemia until his neighbor, Joe, let it slip as we were sitting in the hospital room. The leukemia was in remission, and Oscar hoped he could beat this one, too. When I visited him, he would bring up the Maness family. "Anything new?" he'd ask.

I shrugged. "I haven't been able to find Henry on any records. There was a George Maness who went to Arkansas, but I haven't found any children for him. There are still some places I can look."

"That's good," he said. "You know, I'd like to go see Thurman Maness."

I didn't know what else we could find out, but I wanted to visit Thurman because he had asked me to. And now it would give Oscar something to look forward to, especially since he didn't get to go the last time. I agreed that we would go as soon as he was feeling up to it.

Oscar made it through his chemo and, much to our family's chagrin, started truck-driving again. He was able to get around and go where he wanted to, but gasped for breath after a short walk, like to the car from the living room. We finally took a trip to Carthage, the county seat of Moore County, on July 24, 2010. We drove to the pharmacy first, to visit Lacy Garner.

We went inside and leaned on the counter while the cashier went to get her boss. Lacy welcomed us and invited us to a small conference room with a round veneer table. We had talked on the phone and by e-mail, but this was our first time meeting in person. Lacy said he was glad to meet us. Oscar had printed out a copy of three pictures for him. Back in 1991, I'd found a tintype of a handsome, striking man stuck in a book that belonged to Mamaw. We'd been hoping it was Thomas Maness, but slowly realized it wasn't. The unlabeled photograph was too pristine, in an uncrumpled paper frame, whereas the tintype of Thomas had been carried around in Paw's wallet, then Papaw's, for many years. One of Oscar's three photos was a dark-haired man, average looking, with a mild-mannered face. Although that didn't seem to fit our potential Casanova with five wives, the corners were well worn. And a picture doesn't always capture the personality.

Tintypes, potential photos of Thomas Maness.[225] *The one on the left bears a resemblance to Thomas Swain Maness' cousin, Tommy P. Maness. The one on the right bears a resemblance to Thomas S. Maness' son, Frank Wiley Maness.*

LACY GARNER AND THURMAN MANESS 97

Lacy gave us copies of two chapters from a book he'd written based on Thurman's oral history. The two had worked as a team on Moore County genealogy over the years. Thurman had gone blind in mid-life, but he remembered stories about the Maness family that dated back to the nineteenth century. Lacy, a genealogy enthusiast,

Tommy P. Maness (Courtesy of Lacy Garner Jr.)

Frank Wiley Maness[226]

Frank Wiley Maness (back row, with mustache) and family[227]

had been Thurman's eyes, writing down the stories. He had sent a sample of Thurman's DNA in to a genealogy company. Although they hadn't found out much from it, he knew that Thurman wouldn't always be around, but the technology would grow.

One of the chapters Lacy gave us was full of tall tales about Thomas Swain Maness. Swain told Reuben, Thurman's father, that he would finish the wounded Yankees off with the butt of his rifle. He considered it a mercy to them. The other chapter told a sweet story about the sacrifice his brother Shadrach had made. The teenage boy had gone into the Confederate Army as a substitute for Quimby Wallace. The young boy had died in battle, but Quimby, a husband and father of two small children, was left alive to provide for his family.[228]

After our visit with Lacy, Oscar and I drove down to Southern Pines after calling ahead to the nursing home. A paper banner across Thurman's door proclaimed "Happy Birthday!" He would turn 101 in a few days, on July 27. He wasn't sitting up, this time, as he could no longer get out of bed easily. He apologized for not getting up.

"No problem," I said, pulling a chair over. It had been a year or two, but it was like we were old friends. I leaned close and let him touch my face. He could see some through his eyes, blurry bits of light and dark, and I knew he wanted to see me as best he could. If Uncle Oscar were surprised, he adjusted.

I reminded him who we were. "I'm the lady from Randolph County, remember? Who might be kin to Thomas Swain Maness."

"Oh, yes. I remember you!" His face lit up and the stories I'd heard before started pouring forth.

CHAPTER 26
DNA GENEALOGY

August 2010

I DIDN'T PROMISE TO VISIT AGAIN, this time, because I had the feeling I wouldn't be able to follow through. A couple of weeks later, I opened my e-mail to see Lacy's name. I knew, before I opened it. Thurman had passed away on Sunday, August 8, 2010.

I wrote up a tribute for my blog, about the sweet man who, blind for the last three decades of his life, had faithfully passed on a century of history, contributing to several books. I was so glad we had gone to visit him.

Lacy gladly provided the name of the company he'd used for Thurman's DNA, Family Tree DNA. He also connected me with a well organized online group that compared Maness family DNA. Oscar and I pitched in together on the cost of the Y-DNA test, used to find or verify male lineage. Since Oscar was Thomas Maness' son's son's son, and Thurman was Swain's father's son's son, we had all-male lines to compare. I eagerly awaited the results.

At an earlier family get-together with our Maness family, one of my older cousins had stood up and began to declare how we were all descended from these Scottish brothers, Shadrach, Meshach and Abednego. No, no, no! I thought. We don't know that for sure — don't start an oral tradition that might be wrong! Yet, I hoped it was true. Here I was, the fourth generation looking for a man who disappeared before his son was born. If the DNA proved a connection between Oscar and Thurman, we'd not only solve the family mystery, we'd also be connected to a long family line from Scotland via Thurman's years of research.

It was a good thing we had signed up with that Maness family DNA group, because I didn't have a clue how to interpret the results when they arrived. Mike, who ran the group, told me he'd have some answers soon. I had to send him information from my great-great-grandmother's marriage certificate, which listed Thomas' parents as George and Mary Maness.

Finally I got an e-mail. Mike had compared the Y-chromosome markers and started a new family group for us. In other words, according to Y-DNA, Uncle Oscar wasn't even remotely related to Thurman Maness.

I was floored. I, who'd warned my extended family not to get their hopes up, had been deep down sure our Thomas Maness and Swain Maness were the same man.

I kept thinking about the movie *Sommersby*, with Richard Gere and Jodie Foster. A character in the movie had taken on the identity of a fellow Confederate soldier who had died in a prison camp. Could Thomas have lied about his parents, his age, even his name? Was our surname, our whole Maness extended family, based on a lie? George and Mary didn't seem to exist anywhere. Could some stranger have met Thomas Swain Maness and taken on his identity, only to change it to someone else in the next town? If so, how would I ever figure out who he really was? I would have to start from scratch.

After sharing the bad news with my uncle and mulling over those same thoughts together, he encouraged me to contact Lacy Garner. I figured he would be just as disappointed. To my surprise, he was encouraging. He reminded me that everything he and Thurman had written about Swain's family, including his father being Henry, and the father dying young and the children taken in by different family members, had been based on oral history. While that oral history was only second-hand — very fresh, as it were — Lacy had never found any written documents to substantiate it. In other words, Swain's parentage had never been proven. He could still be our man. I thought that was a long shot.

Besides DNA genealogy, one of the huge changes in technology during the past decade was Facebook. Through social networking, I kept in touch with a couple of my Maness cousins whom I otherwise would have seen only at funerals and rare reunions. My cousin Becky, Paw's granddaughter, sent me a private message asking how the search was going. I typed a short reply, expressing my disappointment in the DNA results.

"That's too bad," Becky replied, then went on: "Daddy always said Thomas was a tall, black-headed man. He was a woodcutter by trade."

As I read Becky's words on the screen, a shiver ran down my back. I hurried to the file cabinet and rifled through papers to find Lacy's stories. I read through the typed papers until I found that part: "He was a mighty fine timberjack. ... Swain Maness could chop down a tree before most men got started."[229] Bless you, Becky! It just had to be him!

CHAPTER 27

MARTHA

Moore County, 1895

Wherever Thomas wandered through the years, he always came back to Moore County, perhaps to visit his sisters. In 1870, Mary Catherine lived with the Bailey family in Carter's Mills, three houses down from a young woman near her age, Martha J. Mashburn. The unmarried Martha, 22 at the time, had an infant daughter named Susan.[230]

Illegitimacy ran in the family; Mashburn was her grandmother Penelope's maiden name. Martha's mother, Faraby Jane, was the eldest of Martin and Penelope Jones' sixteen children. She alternately gave her surname as Mashburn or Jones. According the 1870 census, Jane was only sixteen years older than Martha. However, the Jones-Mashburn women tended to get "younger" with every record, especially Martha. A few consistent records indicate she was born around 1849, about the same age as Thomas Maness.[231]

Martha had three children by 1879, at least one of them fathered by Neill McIntosh, a young farmer who lived nearby. Whether 23-year-old Neill McIntosh was in love with Martha or not, he did not marry another woman until he was in his 40s, in 1901.[232]

Thomas and Martha had probably known each other off and on at least twenty-five years, if not their whole lives. Like Thomas, she'd grown up without a father, but near a huge extended family. She'd had three children out of wedlock, and constantly fibbed about her age. Thomas had met his match.

They were married Oct. 6, 1895, by the Justice of the Peace at her uncle Chris Jones' house in Mount Carmel, Bensalem township, Moore County. Martha gave her mother's name as Jane Jones and said she didn't know who her father was. She must have laughed — when asked her age for the marriage license, she shaved off fifteen years.[233]

Thomas, however, didn't have any reason to lie. He gave his age as 45, consistent with other marriage records and about the same real age as Martha. He'd had to pretend to be older when he was a boy, but now he really was older. And anybody who cared about his parentage was long gone. What the heck! When asked who his parents were, he answered: George Hunsucker and Polly Maness.[234]

Maness-Mashburn marriage license[235]

CHAPTER 28

SARAH

Highfalls, Moore County, 1901

Sometime around the turn of the century, Thomas took up with Sarah Brady, who lived near Highfalls in upper Moore County. She was the oldest girl in a large farming family. Bradley Brady had married her great-aunt, Catherine Brady (possibly his first cousin), but Sarah probably never knew Bradley.[236] At twenty-two, she was nearly three decades younger than Thomas. Tall and blue-eyed, he must have been either attractive or charming, or both. Or maybe the women in the poor, agricultural South that had lost so many men to the war they simply longed for a man to take care of them. That dream of security was not a good bet for the women in Thomas' life.

Sarah had a baby girl, Cora Etta, on October 1, 1901. Two months later, on December 16, Thomas "made an honest woman" out of her and married her at the Justice of the Peace's house in Ritters Township.[237]

Thomas' other wives were all still living. Up until now, he had married women in different counties or states who never knew about each other. But he had married Martha Mashburn in Mount Carmel, only sixteen miles away from Highfalls. At least two of her daughters had married and moved to other counties, but Martha's whereabouts in the early twentieth century are unknown; she might have remained in Moore County.[238] Moore is a "burned county," and the limited surviving divorce records don't include any mention of Thomas or Martha. How did Thomas get away with having two wives so close together? His extended family must have known. He might have even bragged about the women to his male kinfolk.

Thomas and Sarah had another little girl, Oppie. Several records list her birth in early 1902, just four months after Cora. Obviously, one of the birth dates must be wrong. Oppie might have been born as late as 1904.[239]

CHAPTER 29
SEARCH FOR THE LIVING

Randolph County, 2011

OSCAR AND I WERE OUT EATING at the local diner, hearty plates of southern food in front of us. He asked if I'd found anything new on the Manesses.

"No. I'm not sure where to go, next. I sure wish we'd gotten the names of Swain's granddaughters in Raleigh."

"That's a good place to look. I'm sure you can find them."

We talked about a couple of other things. He liked to share which banks and bonds were giving the best interest — something my mother would have been interested in, but usually made my eyes glaze over. "Did you get your results back from the doctor?" I asked, popping a piece of fried okra into my mouth.

"Yeah," he drawled, looking down at the table.

I swallowed my mouthful of food. "Not good?"

"Not good, honey. I gotta go another round."

That night, I knelt on the floor. I asked God to be with Oscar, my usual kind of short prayer. I'm not usually one to ask for healing, or changing the plans of the Lord of the Universe, because I know we can't live here on earth forever. But I asked him for a little help. People said I was smart, though in college and the engineering world I had learned there were plenty of people smarter than I. "Lord, if you've given me any smarts, if this is my gift at all, help me solve this puzzle. Dear Lord, help me find Thomas Maness — in time for Uncle Osc." I crawled into bed and closed my eyes.

★ ★ ★

I BRAINSTORMED IDEAS INTO MY NOTEBOOK. There were three possiblilities: One: Our ancestor, Thomas S. Maness, was telling the truth, information on the marriage license and the oral history of what he had told my family. Two: He was partially lying: he really was Thomas Maness but had lied about his parents and maybe other details. Or three: He was completely lying, and wasn't even a Maness! I left blanks after each option as I wrote them down, then took a deep breath and started answering the question of what I could do in each case.

The truth. He really went to Virginia. He could have married someone else and simply never come back. Or he could have died en route as a John Doe. In that case, I needed to restart my pursuit of his parents, George and Mary Maness. There was a George in secondary sources who went to Arkansas but was too old; I could follow his trail and try to find descendants, perhaps a son named George.

Partial truth. He could still be Swain Maness. First, I could find records of Swain's other marriages and cross-check the information, including parents. Second, I could track down any of Swain's descendants. DNA testing required a straight male line or a female line. But I kept hoping a descendant, no matter what gender, might have a photo of him to compare with the tintypes we had that might be Thomas. I could also check other records — military, court — anything that might mention his parents, birthdate or birthplace. Speaking of military, I could look up Swain's brothers for mentions of family. So many records to check! The whole strategy focused on Swain.

All lies. What if our Thomas had lied about everything, and wasn't even a Maness! My only hope came from DNA, opening up the search to non-Maness matches. With so many surnames in the Y-DNA matches, I hoped this last possibility wasn't the case.

As I organized everything I had found about Thomas Maness over the past two decades, I ran across that slip of yellow paper with the name and phone number of the man from the Maness reunion on it, Don McCaskill. It seemed my best chance of breaking through the Thomas Maness brick wall was to find Swain Maness' granddaughters by his last wife, the ones Thurman had met years ago. Maybe Don could provide a clue. Nervous, I dialed the phone number, wondering if it had changed in all this time. He answered the phone, still at the same number. I explained who I was, a possible relative of Thomas Swain Maness.

"Thomas McSwain Maness, oh, yes," he recalled.

I ventured, "Do you know if Thomas Maness and Sarah Brady had any children?"

The sound of a clacking keyboard traveled through the phone. "Yes, they had a child named Cora. Cora married a man named Herbert Brown and they lived in Johnston County." He kindly directed me to the Randolph Room in Asheboro, the nearest library that had a copy of his book.

I drove down to Asheboro later that week. The version of the Maness book they had was indeed a few years old. Don's book was in a binder, the kind that, instead of first or second editions, changed every time he printed out new pages. I copied the pages with Thomas McSwain and Sarah Brady Maness and their daughter Cora. Although all the sources gave S. for a middle name, oral history had influenced secondary sources to use McSwain.

I found Cora and her family on the census, then her and her husband's death certificates. I searched online for Cora's address, to see which newspaper might have run an obituary. An actual photo of her house popped up, as it had been listed for sale on a realty site. Just for the serendipity of it, I printed out the listing. The library borrowed microfilm of the newspaper, and voilà! Cora's obituary listed her three daughters, with married names, and where they lived in 1994. Two had moved to other states, but one of them still lived in Raleigh: Lessie Williams.

The research trail now ran through the twentieth century, with its more generous death records and obituaries. One of the genealogists

I followed online, Randy Seaver, provided some resources for finding the living on his Genea-Musings blog, including a search engine called Spokeo. I looked up Cora's daughters and found a mix of helpful information and errors. For example, Spokeo listed me with the correct age, an old address, and said that I lived with my late mother. We hadn't lived together since I was in high school.

I called Myrtle, first. I hated calling strangers. Would she think I was some kind of scammer? Would she hang up on me?

She answered. My mouth was already talking before I remembered my manners. My family had been laughing over Thomas Swain Maness' possible escapades and multiple wives for years. But now I was talking to a potential granddaughter, who might have inherited a nobler perspective. I told her that I might be one of his descendants. I was looking for confirmation and any information about him she might have.

Myrtle was completely nice about it, but didn't know much about her grandfather. "He died before I was born," she said. "My older sister would know more about it. You should talk to her." She kindly gave me Lessie's name and phone number, the same number Spokeo had listed.

I dialed Lessie's number and listened to an old-fashioned ring. She picked up and answered warily. I could certainly understand. After I told her about my conversation with her sister and what I wanted, she warmed up.

"Yes, my grandfather's name was Thomas Maness," she said. "He was in the Civil War."

My hopes started to rise. "Do you have any pictures of him?" I asked.

"No. Momma's house burned down way back, and everything like that was lost."

My hopes plummeted. When I asked her if she knew anything about him, she agreed he was from Moore County, but he had died when her mother was just a baby.

"She didn't know him. So I can't tell you much," she said.

I was disappointed. But Lessie gave me one more tidbit of information. I had never found anything on Sarah Brady after Thomas' death, and we had assumed she died young. Lessie told me her grandmother was mentioned in a book a relative had written about the Brady family. I found a copy in Asheboro. The information in it eventually led to a death record and obituary. Thomas Swain Maness' last wife not only outlived him, she remarried, had more children, and lived until 1964. I hadn't been able to find Sarah Maness because she had become Sarah Jones. And her death certificate? The address matched the realty listing for the little house in Raleigh. She'd lived her final days at her daughter Cora's house.

CHAPTER 30
BACK TO DNA
March 2012

I was happy to find Lessie and wanted to meet her sometime, but I didn't know where to go next to connect our Thomas with Swain Maness. Should I try to find Swain's sister's descendants and see if anybody had a photograph? I had recently discovered that many of them lived in Randolph County, but there were so many, it would be like looking for a needle in a haystack. Census records showed Maness families in Tennessee, Kentucky, and Arkansas. Should I trace them for any truth in our Thomas saying he was from Arkansas — even though he said Moore County on Pandora's marriage certificate? I was overwhelmed.

Trying to make sense of my jumbled thoughts, I grabbed a piece of paper and drew a family tree of Swain's family. I used a highlighter to trace branches that had come up as DNA matches with each other. The visual branches showed that Thurman, with whom we originally compared our DNA, was definitely in the Maness family — no unknown illegitimacy among his "known" ancestors. In contrast, neither Swain, nor his reputed father Henry, had had any descendants tested.

The following spring, in March 2012, I read about a new test, autosomal DNA. Because it had nothing to do with the sex chromosomes or the mitochondrial DNA (which is passed down only from mothers), you couldn't tell which parent it came from. The autosomal DNA test, nicknamed the "Family Finder" test, compared strings of genetic code, looking for identical sequences between family members. Since the DNA gets more jumbled through the generations, the test only works on close relatives — no more than third cousins.

I pulled out my hand-drawn family tree. I'd crowded a lot of names onto the normal sized piece of copy paper, so I saw Sarah Brady's name and her daughters not far from Thurman's family. Just for fun, I started figuring up levels of cousins. If Swain was really Thomas, Thurman and Paw would be second cousins, making him and Oscar second cousins, twice removed.

I looked at Cora's name, written under Sarah. She'd be ... wait, not a cousin. She'd be Paw's half-sister! That blew my mind. But yes, if Swain kept marrying younger women as he grew older, he had children, siblings, who were more than 36 years apart. Like a generation apart, but really in the same generation. So Lessie and Papaw would be first cousins. And Lessie and Oscar, two living people, would be first cousins, once removed. In other words, close kin. Closer than I'd ever imagined after a century of generations. Close enough to take the autosomal DNA test.

The test was new and cost $289. I called Family Tree DNA and verified that we would indeed need two tests to compare, as the previous one with my uncle had been a different kind. I talked it over with Oscar.

"If this'll give us the answer, let's do it!" he said. He offered to pay half.

I called Lessie. After so many months, she didn't remember me. But after I explained, she agreed to take the DNA test.

As we waited for the results, I wrote updates on my genealogy and books blog. A couple of cousins read the posts and wrote encouraging notes. I drove up to Maryland to visit friends for the weekend. I stayed with my friend Suzy, who let me use her internet. After visiting friends and resting, I checked e-mail on Saturday afternoon. There was a message from Family Tree DNA.

I routinely got matches through Uncle Oscar's account. This message wasn't for Oscar. It was addressed to Lessie. I logged in, for the first time as Lessie, then clicked on the Family Finder results. The default was set to close relatives, like first to second cousins. There was only one name in Lessie's close relatives list — Frank Oscar Maness.

It's him! I whooped. We found Thomas Maness! Thomas and Swain were the same man, and now I had proof. I pulled out my cell phone to call my uncle.

CHAPTER 31
FINAL TALL TALE

Robbins, Moore County, December 24, 1903

Thomas may have been called "Tom" when he was younger. Sometime in his later life, especially in Moore County, he became known by his middle name, "Swain." Perhaps it was to tell him apart from Tommy P. Maness, his presumed first cousin and Thurman's grandfather.

Thomas' history shows he was a restless man. There aren't any stories that tell how he got along with his wives when he was home. But in 1903, he didn't spend Christmas Eve with Sarah and their two little girls (or one little girl, Cora, as Sarah might have been pregnant with Oppie). Instead, he went to see Ira Maness that evening, in or near Robbins. They sat and talked. Finally Ira went on to bed, leaving Thomas in the rocking chair.

Ira got up the next morning and found him still sitting there. Dead.

Ira went to Pleasant Hill Church and rang the bell. Reuben Maness, Tommy P.'s son and a minister (nephew of Rev. Reuben Maness who died in Petersburg), lived behind the church. He walked up to the church and asked, "What's wrong, Ary?"

"Swain's dead." Ira told him the story.

"What do you plan on doing?" Reuben asked.

"I want to bury him."

"You ain't planning on burying him, today, are you?"

"Yes. I'm a'gonna bury him today."

They rang the bell again. All the church folks that lived around knew something had happened. The men folk made their way to the church and gathered around, wondering what in the world it was. Reuben told them, "Swain Maness is dead, and Ary wants to bury him today."

"Today? It's Christmas!" the men complained.

Ira insisted. He wanted to get him out of the house. They discussed where to bury him. He'd been in trouble with the law and hadn't been the most upstanding member of the community. They decided to bury him in the woods near the church, not in the actual cemetery with the "good folks."

The men started digging. The morning was bitter cold, and as they dug, they took nips from the flasks or Christmas bottles they'd brought with them. They dug and drank, dug and drank, until they had an unusually deep hole in the ground. About that time, Ira drove up in a wagon. He had found or made a box and put Swain's body in it. Reuben helped him carry the coffin to the gravesite, snagging his pants on the way.

The story goes that the hole was so deep, that when they dropped the coffin in, everybody stood around the edge, waiting to hear it hit bottom.

Laughing and talking and almost falling over drunk, the men filled in the hole. Reuben hated to see Swain buried like a dog. So he quieted the men and threw a handful of dirt over the grave. Reuben asked the Lord if he would take Swain's soul and take care of him. Then everybody went on home.

The author at Thomas Swain Maness' grave in 2015

Reuben kept up the grave for many years. Eventually, the cemetery grew around it, so now Thomas Swain Maness is in the churchyard with everybody else.[240]

LEGACY

BROTHERS AND SISTERS AND BROTHERS IN ARMS

According to the oral history, Henry Maness had six children, most with rhyming names: Lundy Jane, Leanda Cain, Alexander Lane, Shadrach Squire Gain, Mary Catherine or Kathryn, and Thomas Swain. Mary Catherine and Thomas were both born around 1850, give or take a year, so it is not known which was older or if they were twins. The story goes that Henry and his unknown wife died young and the children went to live with various family members. The only record that connects any of them to each other is when Alexander and Mary Catherine lived with Ira Maness (Henry's first cousin) in the 1860 census. Young Shadrach was living with Quimby Wallace in another part of Moore County.[241]

Thomas' sisters worked as servants with various families in upper Moore County in 1870.[242] Then they disappear from the records. No marriage or death record has been found for Lundy Jane, Leanda Cain or Mary Catherine (although Mary Manesses abound, none are a confirmed match). Not only does the lost 1890 federal census confound the search, the Moore County Courthouse burned in 1889. More records were lost in an early-twentieth-century courthouse flood.[243]

Thomas' only known nephew was Hugh Alexander Maness, Lundy Jane's son. Hugh grew up with the Buie family and lived next door to the two spinster sisters as an adult. Whether his mother found another job and moved out, married, or died remains a mystery. An ambiguous marking on Hugh's marriage license implies that she passed away before 1892.[244]

Hugh married Mary Jane McCaskill and they had seven children: Ida Lee Hicks, Mary L. Grant, Daniel Alexander Maness Sr., James Calvin "Callie" Maness, William Clay Maness, Katherine Mae Beane, and Pearl Estelle Shaw. Hugh worked at a saw mill, tried a stint at farming, then went back to mill work as a "fireman" for the steam engine. In later life, he and Mary moved to Asheboro in Randolph County and took in boarders. Hugh passed away January 10, 1939, at age 72. Mary Jane died just over a month later, February 18. Many of their descendants live in Randolph and Guilford counties.[245]

Alexander died March 3, 1868, purportedly from wounds suffered during the war, but his military records don't mention him being wounded. Possibly the effects of living in the POW camp deteriorated his health. He was 23 years old.[246]

Shadrach's body remained in an unmarked grave in Petersburg. Some years later, Thurman Maness erected a tombstone in his memory in the Pleasant Hill Methodist Church cemetery in Moore County.[247] Quimby and Arabella Wallace had eight more children, for a total of ten. In addition to William Wesley and Martha A., they had Nancy, Rufus, Charlotte, Eli, Eliza Alice, James L., Jesse Lewis, and Bettie.[248] At least seven of the children, not to mention their families and grandchildren, wouldn't have existed without Shadrach's sacrifice. Ira Maness' mother was a Wallace, and his first cousin, the mysterious Henry

Alexander's grave

Brothers and Sisters

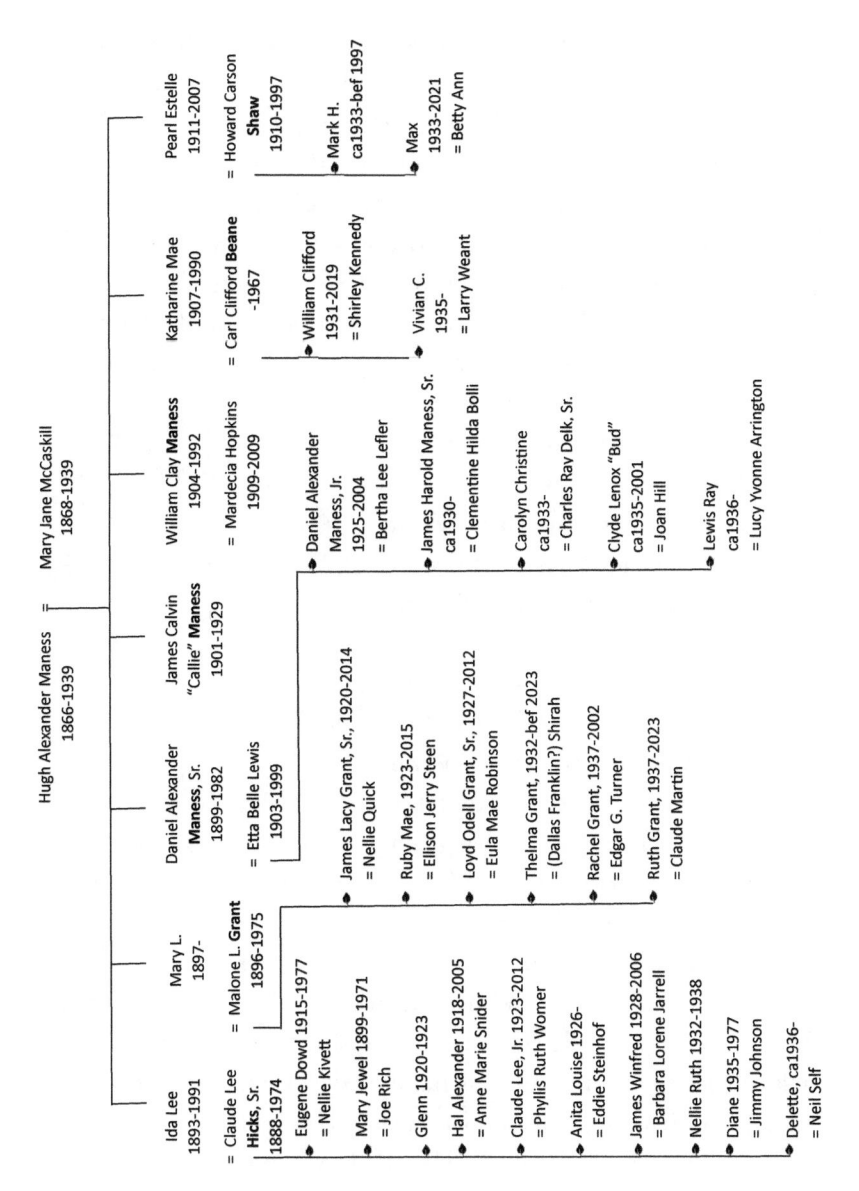

Hugh Alexander Maness 1866-1939 = Mary Jane McCaskill 1868-1939

- Ida Lee 1893-1991
  = Claude Lee Hicks, Sr. 1888-1974
- Mary L. 1897-
  = Malone L. **Grant** 1896-1975
  - Eugene Dowd 1915-1977
    = Nellie Kivett
  - Mary Jewel 1899-1971
    = Joe Rich
  - Glenn 1920-1923
  - Hal Alexander 1918-2005
    = Anne Marie Snider
  - Claude Lee, Jr. 1923-2012
    = Phyllis Ruth Womer
  - Anita Louise 1926-
    = Eddie Steinhof
  - James Winfred 1928-2006
    = Barbara Lorene Jarrell
  - Nellie Ruth 1932-1938
  - Diane 1935-1977
    = Jimmy Johnson
  - Delette, ca1936-
    = Neil Self
- Daniel Alexander **Maness**, Sr. 1899-1982
  = Etta Belle Lewis 1903-1999
  - James Lacy Grant, Sr., 1920-2014
    = Nellie Quick
  - Ruby Mae, 1923-2015
    = Ellison Jerry Steen
  - Loyd Odell Grant, Sr., 1927-2012
    = Eula Mae Robinson
  - Thelma Grant, 1932-bef 2023
    = (Dallas Franklin?) Shirah
  - Rachel Grant, 1937-2002
    = Edgar G. Turner
  - Ruth Grant, 1937-2023
    = Claude Martin
- James Calvin "Callie" **Maness** 1901-1929
- William Clay **Maness** 1904-1992
  = Mardecia Hopkins 1909-2009
  - Daniel Alexander Maness, Jr. 1925-2004
    = Bertha Lee Lefler
  - James Harold Maness, Sr. ca1930-
    = Clementine Hilda Bolli
  - Carolyn Christine ca1933-
    = Charles Ray Delk, Sr.
  - Clyde Lenox "Bud" ca1935-2001
    = Joan Hill
  - Lewis Ray ca1936-
    = Lucy Yvonne Arrington
- Katharine Mae 1907-1990
  = Carl Clifford **Beane** -1967
  - William Clifford 1931-2019
    = Shirley Kennedy
  - Vivian C. 1935-
    = Larry Weant
- Pearl Estelle 1911-2007
  = Howard Carson **Shaw** 1910-1997
  - Mark H. ca1933-bef 1997
  - Max 1933-2021
    = Betty Ann

Hugh A. Maness Family Tree[249]

Maness, was rumored to have married a Wallace. So Quimby and the Maness siblings were probably related. (Quimby's relatives and the author's family are distant relations according to autosomal DNA.)

Oral history says that after Quimby died (before July 1900), Arabella claimed a small pension based on Shadrach's service. North Carolina pension application records, however, show nothing to back up that story. Arabella lived to the age of 92, passing away in 1928.[250]

Jonas Sedberry Maness had survived being shot through the jaw during the Battle of Gettysburg and returned to duty for nearly a year. He was finally retired to the "Invalid Corps" on September 29, 1864. Sedberry wore a beard to cover the scar and retained a speech impediment. After the war, he married and had seven children. Like other farmers in the devastated South, he struggled to survive. He packed up his family and moved to Randolph County to work in the growing textile industry. They later moved to Eden, near the Virginia line, where Sedberry died in 1898.[251]

Jonas Sedberry Maness (Courtesy of Beth Maness)[252]

Like Sedberry, Bradley Brady survived his wounds and returned to duty in the Twenty-Sixth Regiment. He was reported Absent Without Leave on July 1, 1864 — not long after Thomas tried to defect to the Union side.[253] Bradley made his way back to Moore County and his family. His wife died by 1870, when Bradley was living with his son Bethuel and his mother in Prosperity.[254] Bradley is presumed to have died by 1880, when Bethuel is living with his grandparents.[255]

Col. John R. Lane had miraculously survived being shot through the neck and jaw at Gettysburg. He then survived shots in the thigh at the Battle of the Wilderness, in his right leg at Yellow Tavern, and in his chest just over the heart at Reams' Station. He returned to duty each time, until his injuries and perhaps the cold weather wore him down late in the war. After a stay in the hospital he was paroled May 2,

1865, and returned home to Chatham County.[256]

Forty years later, at a reunion at Gettysburg, he said that "a Yankee bullet ruined my throat and took away a part of my tongue and deprived me of my teeth." He went on to proudly tell the story of the Twenty-Sixth Regiment. He shook hands with Charles H. McConnell, then sergeant of the Michigan "Iron Brigade," who had taken careful aim with his last cartridge at the man holding the flag, forty years earlier on the same field.[257]

John R. Lane[258]

THE MAYNOR FAMILY

Thomas' first wife, Mary Craton (sometimes Crayton) Maness, worked on or around farms all her life, listed as a milk maid in the 1900 census.[259] Her two boys changed their surname to Maynor later in life. Mary likely never knew what happened to Thomas. She called herself a widow and never remarried. She lived for many years with her older son, William Nuton, and his family.[260] She died September 12, 1915, at age 75, and is buried somewhere in Orange United Methodist Church's cemetery in Chapel Hill.[261] Her daughter, Martha, was still alive in 1910, but her married name is unknown.[262]

William Nuton Maynor and his wife, Mollie, worked on a dairy farm. They had eight children, seven of whom lived to adulthood. Three of those never married, and three married but no children have been found in available records. More on the youngest two later.[263]

Mary's and Thomas' other son, James Robert "Bob" Maynor, was very tall, about six and a half feet. He also worked on a farm. He married Lula Mincey, who was around five feet tall and probably weighed less than a hundred pounds. "She dipped snuff with a tree stem," said her granddaughter, Gail Gordon. Lula had a little dog and doted on it.[264]

They had nine children, with many descendants still in the Chapel Hill area of Orange and Chatham counties. One of their older grandchildren, Theodore Blackwood, married William Nuton's youngest daughter, Floy Valentine Maynor — his first cousin, once removed.

Robert and Lula Maynor[265]    *Lula Maynor with her dog (All courtesy of Gail Gordon)*[266]

Theodore's sister, Lavear Beatrice Blackwood, married William Nuton's youngest son. These two couples had children, and so William Nuton's only descendants are part of his brother's family tree.[267]

Bob Maynor died November 19, 1952, age 83. Lula lived to be 102, passing away August 30, 1974. Her obituary listed their descendants at that time: "38 grandchildren, 85 great-grandchildren, 88 great-great-grandchildren, and six great-great-great-grandchildren."[268]

THE MAYNOR FAMILY

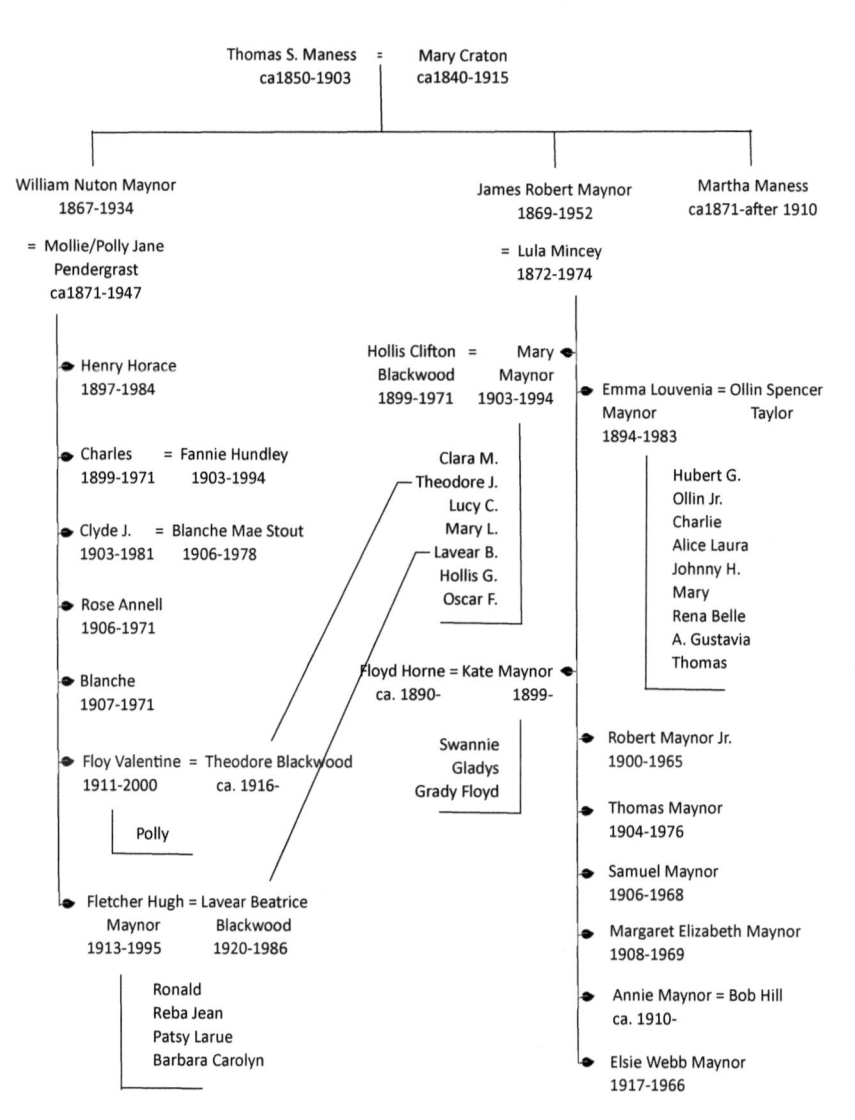

```
Thomas S. Maness  =  Mary Craton
ca1850-1903          ca1840-1915
```

William Nuton Maynor
1867-1934

= Mollie/Polly Jane
Pendergrast
ca1871-1947

- Henry Horace
  1897-1984

- Charles   = Fannie Hundley
  1899-1971   1903-1994

- Clyde J.   = Blanche Mae Stout
  1903-1981   1906-1978

- Rose Annell
  1906-1971

- Blanche
  1907-1971

- Floy Valentine = Theodore Blackwood
  1911-2000   ca. 1916-

  Polly

- Fletcher Hugh = Lavear Beatrice
  Maynor   Blackwood
  1913-1995   1920-1986

  Ronald
  Reba Jean
  Patsy Larue
  Barbara Carolyn

James Robert Maynor
1869-1952

= Lula Mincey
1872-1974

Hollis Clifton = Mary
Blackwood   Maynor
1899-1971   1903-1994

Clara M.
Theodore J.
Lucy C.
Mary L.
Lavear B.
Hollis G.
Oscar F.

Floyd Horne = Kate Maynor
ca. 1890-   1899-

Swannie
Gladys
Grady Floyd

- Emma Louvenia = Ollin Spencer
  Maynor   Taylor
  1894-1983

  Hubert G.
  Ollin Jr.
  Charlie
  Alice Laura
  Johnny H.
  Mary
  Rena Belle
  A. Gustavia
  Thomas

- Robert Maynor Jr.
  1900-1965

- Thomas Maynor
  1904-1976

- Samuel Maynor
  1906-1968

- Margaret Elizabeth Maynor
  1908-1969

- Annie Maynor = Bob Hill
  ca. 1910-

- Elsie Webb Maynor
  1917-1966

Martha Maness
ca1871-after 1910

Maynor Family Tree[269]

OUR MANESS CLAN

Thomas Maness' second wife, Pandora, worked in domestic service, including a year up until April 1886 in the kitchen of the McAdoo House (later hotel) on South Elm Street in Greensboro. She had a white horse for transportation, and worked at the O. Henry Hotel, which opened in Greensboro in 1919.

When her son, Franklin Wiley Maness, was twenty years old, he went to Virginia to look for his father. Nobody he met knew any-

O. Henry Hotel[270]

136　THE SEARCH FOR THOMAS MANESS

Pandora's signature

Four generations: Sarah Pandora Wall Maness (left), Frank Wiley Maness, and Martha Gossett Wall Chappell with Frank's first child, Pearl Maness[271]

OUR MANESS CLAN 137

Five generations: Frank Wiley Maness with Sam Franklin, Martha Gossett Wall Chappell, Pandora Wall Maness, and Pearl Maness Franklin[272]

Maness family (from left): Florence Maness, Bessie Maness, John and Treva Presnell Maness, Annie Maness Andrews, Daisy Routh and Frank Vance Maness, Frank Wiley Maness, Annie's friend, Emma English Maness, Mary Maness, and (maybe) Margaret Andrews[273]

Frank Vance and Daisy Maness with Florence (center), Bessie (right) and Oscar[275]

thing about him. He carried a tintype photo of Thomas in his wallet. Every time he met someone with the name Maness, he asked if they knew him. Pandora never knew what happened to Thomas. In later years she called herself a widow, but she never remarried.[274] Her mother, Martha Chappell, outlived her second husband, living to the great old age of 98, but losing sight due to an eyelid condition. The two women kept house together, living in Archdale on the Randolph-Guilford county line.

Pandora's baby sister, Mary Jane, also outlived two husbands, whom she buried at the Methodist Church on Fairfield Road in Archdale. The three women, however — Martha, Pandora and Mary Jane — are buried together at Centre Friends Meeting cemetery, even though none of them were Quaker. As previously mentioned, they grew up in the Centre community and the daughters might have attended Quaker schools.[276] Pandora passed away July 30, 1930, at 70 years old.[277]

Frank Wiley Maness, known as "Paw" to his children and grandchildren, was a farmer all his life. He married a Quaker woman named Emma English and joined the Religious Society of Friends, Springfield Friends Meeting. He helped build a new meetinghouse in Archdale in the early twentieth century, hauling bricks in his wagon. Paw and his wife had seven children, six of whom lived to adulthood and had families.[278]

One of those children was Frank Vance Maness, who also asked every Maness he met about his missing grandfather. He was a bird dog trainer who helped train nationally recognized dogs. He and his uncle and cousins worked as hunting guides for rich men from the north and managed their southern estates, remnants of the gilded

A reunion of Frank Wiley Maness' descendants in 2007. His grandchildren are seated in the second row: (from left) Philip Maness, Rebecca "Becky" Maness Poteat, (Florence's husband, Jim Dale), Florence Maness Dale, John W. Maness, and Oscar Maness.

age. Part of the story of his son Oscar and granddaughter Beth is told in the memoir chapters of this book. Frank and his brother, John, were both tall and slim. Frank, six foot, two inches tall, married Daisy Routh, who was five feet even.

John Maness' children and grandchildren continue the family tradition by raising game birds and hosting hunters at Shady Knoll Gamebird Farm near Asheboro. Frank Wiley Maness' many descendants live in upper Randolph and Davidson counties.

Thomas S. Maness = Sarah Pandora Wall
ca1850-1903   1859-1930

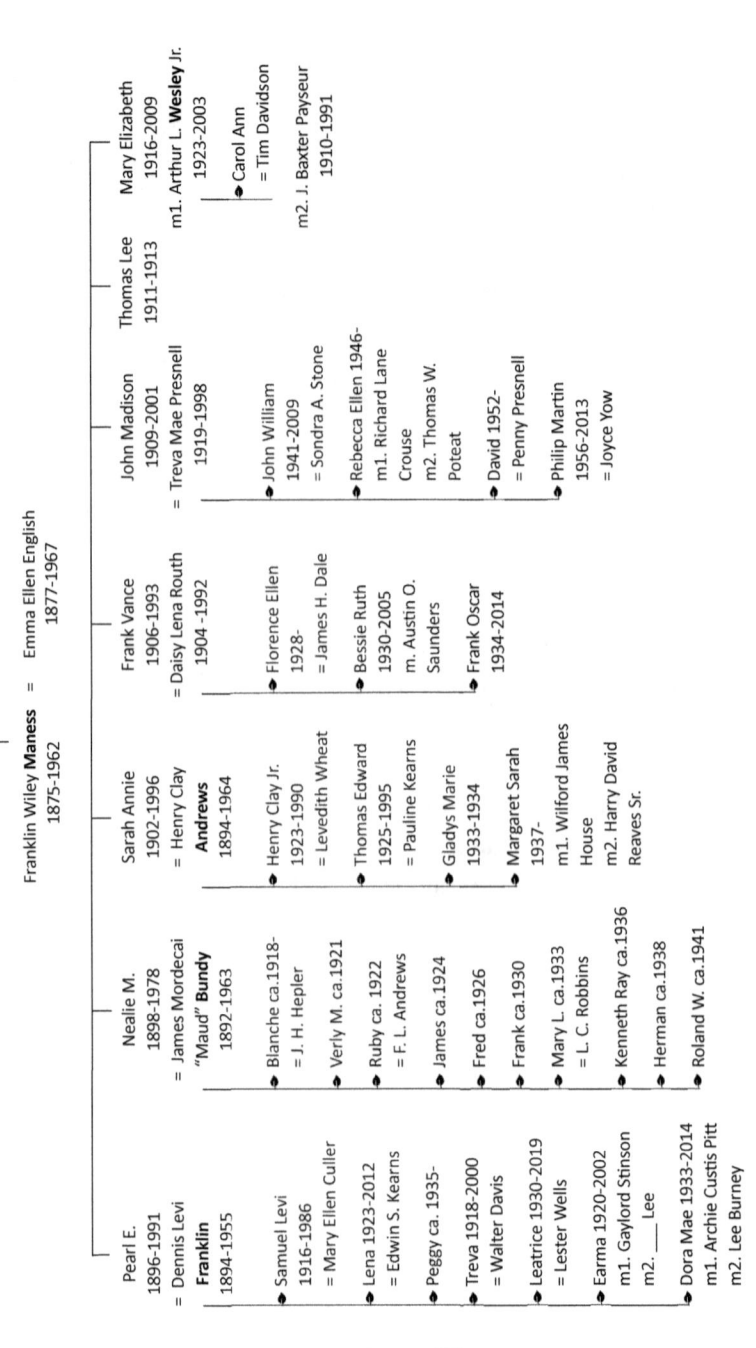

Franklin Wiley **Maness** = Emma Ellen English
1875-1962   1877-1967

Children of Franklin Wiley Maness and Emma Ellen English:

Pearl E. 1896-1991
= Dennis Levi **Franklin** 1894-1955

- Samuel Levi 1916-1986
  = Mary Ellen Culler
- Lena 1923-2012
  = Edwin S. Kearns
- Peggy ca. 1935-
- Treva 1918-2000
  = Walter Davis
- Leatrice 1930-2019
  = Lester Wells
- Earma 1920-2002
  m1. Gaylord Stinson
  m2. ___ Lee
- Dora Mae 1933-2014
  m1. Archie Custis Pitt
  m2. Lee Burney

Nealie M. 1898-1978
= James Mordecai "**Maud**" **Bundy** 1892-1963

- Blanche ca.1918-
  = J. H. Hepler
- Verly M. ca.1921
- Ruby ca. 1922
  = F. L. Andrews
- James ca.1924
- Fred ca.1926
- Frank ca.1930
- Mary L. ca.1933
  = L. C. Robbins
- Kenneth Ray ca.1936
- Herman ca.1938
- Roland W. ca.1941

Sarah Annie 1902-1996
= Henry Clay **Andrews** 1894-1964

- Henry Clay Jr. 1923-1990
  = Levedith Wheat
- Thomas Edward 1925-1995
  = Pauline Kearns
- Gladys Marie 1933-1934
- Margaret Sarah 1937-
  m1. Wilford James House
  m2. Harry David Reaves Sr.

Frank Vance 1906-1993
= Daisy Lena Routh 1904-1992

- Florence Ellen 1928-
  = James H. Dale
- Bessie Ruth 1930-2005
  m. Austin O. Saunders
- Frank Oscar 1934-2014

John Madison 1909-2001
= Treva Mae Presnell 1919-1998

- John William 1941-2009
  = Sondra A. Stone
- Rebecca Ellen 1946-
  m1. Richard Lane Crouse
  m2. Thomas W. Poteat
- David 1952-
  = Penny Presnell
- Philip Martin 1956-2013
  = Joyce Yow

Thomas Lee 1911-1913

Mary Elizabeth 1916-2009
m1. Arthur L. **Wesley** Jr. 1923-2003

- Carol Ann
  = Tim Davidson

m2. J. Baxter Payseur 1910-1991

Maness Family Tree[279]

THE MANES-SIFFORD FAMILY

Like Pandora, Thomas' third wife supported herself through domestic service. Nancy Pool Maness worked as a housekeeper and reared her two children, Fannie Betty and Thomas Cleveland, in Giles County, Virginia. She was working as a maid for the Porterfield family in 1900. Some time after that she moved to Pulaski County, Virginia, and worked as a housekeeper into her sixties.[280]

Fannie Maness married Charles Sifford, a railroad worker who came from an old family that had settled the New River area. They had six children. Cleveland grew up to work in the coal mines. In West Virginia, he married an English immigrant named Agnes Swabey. They, too, had six children. Their surname changed to Manes. After a stint in Ohio, Cleveland and his family moved to Canonsburg, Pennsylvania.[281]

Nancy owned a cottage house in Belspring, a rural community on the New River, just north of Radford in Pulaski County. A 1918 photograph of a crowd in the nearby town of Pulaski at a Christmas celebration shows women wearing hats of her era, their coats buttoned tightly against the December chill. The picture shows a horse and buggy as well as a Model T car.

142 THE SEARCH FOR THOMAS MANESS

Christmas in Pulaski, Virginia, December 1918[282]

Detail, Christmas in Pulaski, 1918

Nancy died suddenly on November 20, 1920. Her death certificate says she was "accidentally killed by train." The tracks run along the river. She must have walked on or near them hundreds of times. The regional newspaper offers no mention of the accident. Her daughter, Fannie, had been fighting tuberculosis for several years. Fannie's husband, Charles, helped officials with Nancy's death as best he could. He knew her by her nickname, Nannie, only knew her father's name, and guessed her age as 67 (she was 66). He didn't know Thomas' name at all. Nancy was buried in Brown's Cemetery, a family plot in Belspring that had gradually grown into a community burying ground. Her grave is unmarked, as are many others. The cemetery sits atop a quiet hill, overlooking a large pasture on one side and the railroad tracks on the other side.[283]

Fannie's long-time illness ended with her death on March 27, 1921, at age 43. She must have filled Charles in about her family in those few months since her mother's death: he listed Fannie's parents as "Thomas Manes" and "Nannie Va. Pool."[284]

They say tragedies sometimes come in threes. Cleveland Manes died unexpectedly of pneumonia April 16, 1924. He was only 37 years old. Back in Virginia, several of Charles Sifford's children (except for one who died young) had grown and moved on to independence. Probably grieved at the double loss of his wife and mother-in-law, and with the financial security and busyness of his railroad job, he had done nothing with Nancy's house. In contrast, Cleveland's widow, Agnes, had six small children and no income. So around 1925, she took Charles to court and forced him to sell Nancy's house. He agreed, but it took several years for court-appointed officials to close out the estate. In the end, each grandchild received around $16 to $25.[285]

Not all of Charles Sifford's children married, but Nannie and Harmon each had five children. Sifford descendants live in Pulaski County to this day.[286]

After a bout with the law as boys, at least two of Agnes' children grew up to distinguish themselves with military careers. Their English-born mother made sure all of the family milestones made it into the local newspaper. Her three girls and three "Manes" boys left descendants in Pennsylvania and other parts of the world, including eighteen grandchildren when Agnes died in 1952.[287]

```
                    Thomas S. Maness    =   Nancy "Nannie" Virginia Pool
                      ca1850-1903                  1854-1920
```

Fannie Betty Maness
1877-1921

= Charles Patton **Sifford**
1874-1941

- May E. Sifford
  1897-1968
  = Christ J. **Mitropulos**

- Loula R. Sifford
  1899-(bef 1910)

- Nannie Ruth Sifford
  1900-1990
  = David E. **Stanton**

- Herman Frank Sifford
  1907-1946
  = Barbara E. Hilton

- Margie Ann Sifford
  1909-1956

- James Boyce Sifford
  1912-1993

Thomas Cleveland Manes
1886-1924

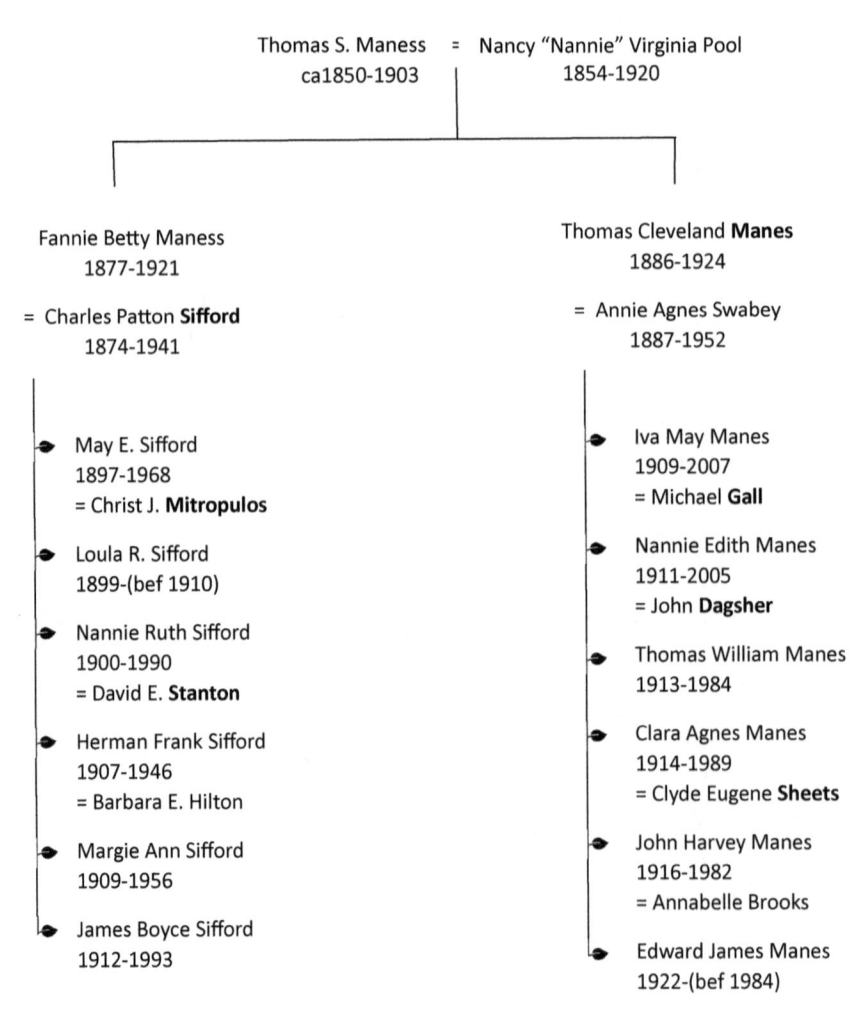

= Annie Agnes Swabey
1887-1952

- Iva May Manes
  1909-2007
  = Michael **Gall**

- Nannie Edith Manes
  1911-2005
  = John **Dagsher**

- Thomas William Manes
  1913-1984

- Clara Agnes Manes
  1914-1989
  = Clyde Eugene **Sheets**

- John Harvey Manes
  1916-1982
  = Annabelle Brooks

- Edward James Manes
  1922-(bef 1984)

Manes-Sifford Family Tree[288]

THE MANERS FAMILY

Louisa Kelly Maness was left on her own with three boys (although the 1900 census said she had four out of six children living). In 1900, she and the two older boys worked as farm labor and rented a house in Lanesboro township, Anson County. Louisa could not read or write, and the family changed their name to Maners.[289] She called herself a widow and managed to marry again, to Samuel Wilbert Atkinson in October 1903. Louisa and Wilbert moved to Gaston County, North Carolina. She died February 26, 1930, at the age of 67.[290]

Herman Fantom "Hampton" Maners, the oldest, grew very tall, about six feet, six inches. His grandson, Martin "Marty" A. Maners Jr., remembers that he had huge hands. Hampton worked for the railroad, laying track, and later became a carpenter. He married Addie Lena Berry in 1906 in Georgia. They had five children and later returned to North Carolina, living in High Point in Guilford County.[291] Lena played the piano. "We all gathered round the piano and sang hymns after lunch," said Marty. When Hampton passed away June 2, 1967, at 80 years old, he had seventeen grandchildren and 27 great-grandchildren.[292]

William Harvey Maners worked in a cotton mill and then an iron works, then later moved to South Carolina and ran a Lincoln-Mercury dealership.[293] He married Ruth Sloan in 1912 in Gastonia, North Carolina. They had four children and four great-grandchildren. Harvey also lived to age 80, dying May 3, 1972.[294]

Herman Fantom Maners with wife, mother, Louisa, and children (Courtesy of Marty Maners)

THE MANERS FAMILY

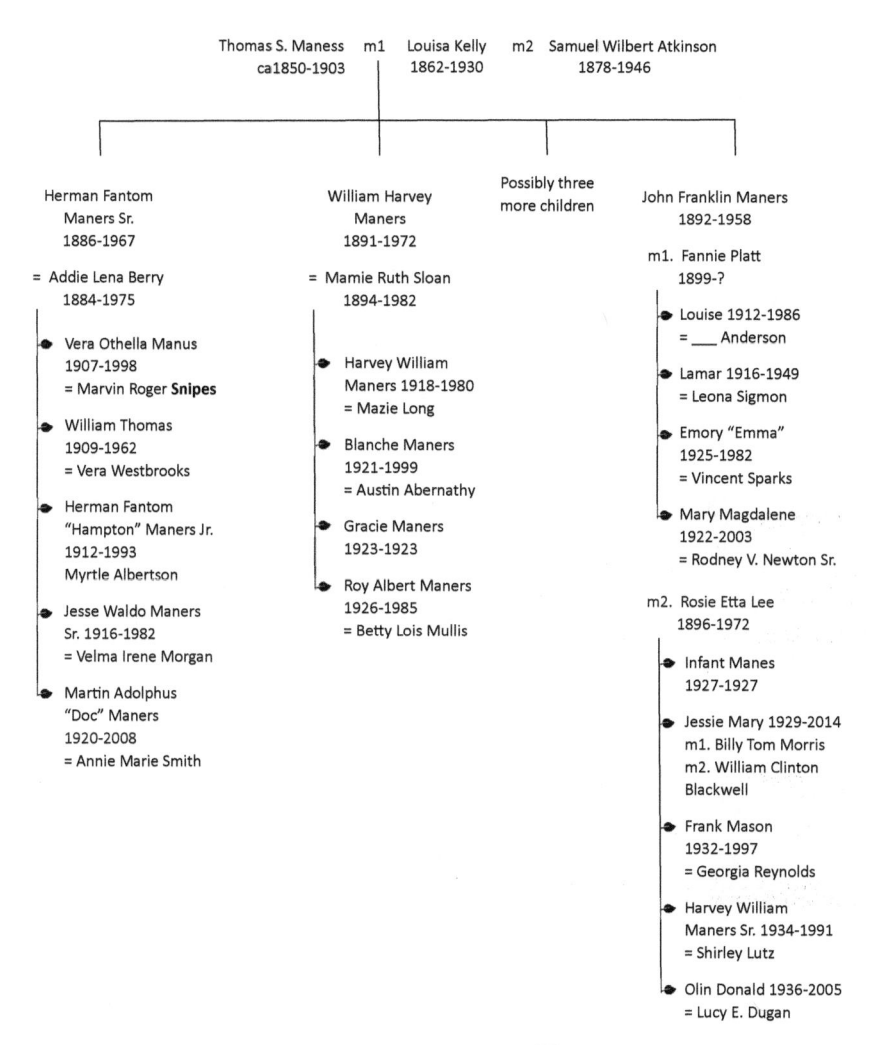

```
Thomas S. Maness   m1   Louisa Kelly   m2   Samuel Wilbert Atkinson
  ca1850-1903              1862-1930              1878-1946
```

- **Herman Fantom Maners Sr.**
  1886-1967
  = Addie Lena Berry
  1884-1975
  - Vera Othella Manus
    1907-1998
    = Marvin Roger **Snipes**
  - William Thomas
    1909-1962
    = Vera Westbrooks
  - Herman Fantom "Hampton" Maners Jr.
    1912-1993
    Myrtle Albertson
  - Jesse Waldo Maners Sr. 1916-1982
    = Velma Irene Morgan
  - Martin Adolphus "Doc" Maners
    1920-2008
    = Annie Marie Smith

- **William Harvey Maners**
  1891-1972
  = Mamie Ruth Sloan
  1894-1982
  - Harvey William Maners 1918-1980
    = Mazie Long
  - Blanche Maners
    1921-1999
    = Austin Abernathy
  - Gracie Maners
    1923-1923
  - Roy Albert Maners
    1926-1985
    = Betty Lois Mullis

- Possibly three more children

- **John Franklin Maners**
  1892-1958
  m1. Fannie Platt
  1899-?
  - Louise 1912-1986
    = ___ Anderson
  - Lamar 1916-1949
    = Leona Sigmon
  - Emory "Emma"
    1925-1982
    = Vincent Sparks
  - Mary Magdalene
    1922-2003
    = Rodney V. Newton Sr.

  m2. Rosie Etta Lee
  1896-1972
  - Infant Manes
    1927-1927
  - Jessie Mary 1929-2014
    m1. Billy Tom Morris
    m2. William Clinton Blackwell
  - Frank Mason
    1932-1997
    = Georgia Reynolds
  - Harvey William Maners Sr. 1934-1991
    = Shirley Lutz
  - Olin Donald 1936-2005
    = Lucy E. Dugan

Maners Family Tree[295]

Frank had nine children, eight of whom lived to adulthood: four with his first wife, Fannie Platt, and five with second wife, Rosie Etta Lee. Frank and Rosie moved from Gaston County to the Charlotte area in Mecklenburg County. He was a painter, working for private contractors for many years. He died August 16, 1958, at 66 years old.[296]

THE MANES-FOREMAN-WALKER FAMILY

WILLIE STEWART'S DAUGHTER, CORA "MANES," NEVER knew her father, Thomas Maness.[297] Willie reared her alone until Cora was ten, then in 1888 Willie married John Thomas Keener, seventeen years her senior. John Keener was a farmer for years, and late in life (into his seventies) he worked as a laborer at a steel plant. Willie had two more children with John, Clara Mae and Willie Sue Keener.[298]

Although her mother couldn't read or write, Cora went to school through the sixth grade. When Cora was seventeen, she married Samuel Walter Foreman, who worked at Gulf States Steel Company. A wedding-day photograph shows the young couple with smiling faces, more natural than the usual formal portrait. Cora and Walter had seven children, three boys and four girls, and lived next to her mother and stepfather in South Gadsden, Alabama.

On January 15, 1923, when the youngest child, Gladys, was a month old, Walter died suddenly in a steel mill explosion.[299] Willie Stewart Manes Keener died February 15, 1929.[300] Later that year, on October 15, 1929, Cora married Thad William Walker, a sharecropper about fifteen years older than she was. They had two more children,

Willie Stewart Manes Keener and John Keener[301]

Cora and Walter Foreman[302]

Cora Manes Foreman Walker (second from right) with children[303]
(All courtesy of Elaine Watts and Mark Skidmore)

Bonnie and Mary Frances Walker. Young Gladys carried her baby sisters to the cotton field for her mother to nurse. Sadly, Thad was in an insane asylum by 1950, the Bryce Hospital in Tuscaloosa, Alabama. He died there in 1952.[304]

Cora lived to the age of 85. When she died April 9, 1974, six of her nine children were still living, as well as "several" grandchildren and great-grandchildren. Some descendants live in Alabama, Virginia and Missouri.[305]

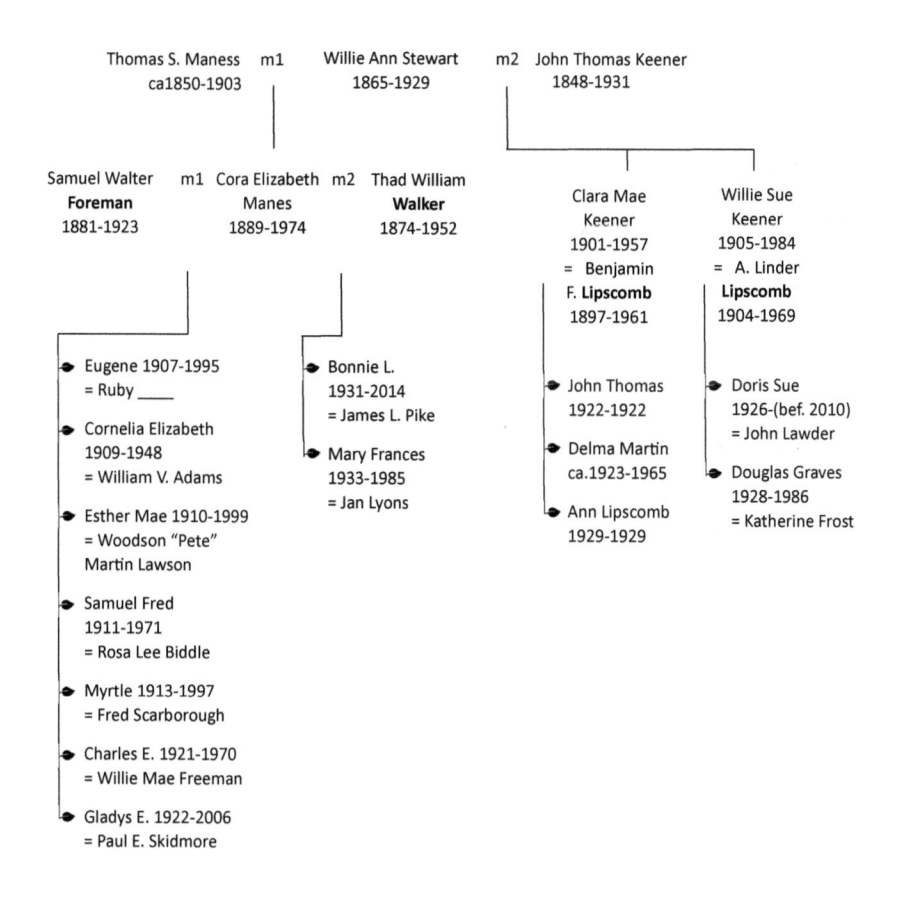

```
Thomas S. Maness   m1   Willie Ann Stewart   m2   John Thomas Keener
    ca1850-1903              1865-1929                1848-1931
```

Samuel Walter   m1   Cora Elizabeth   m2   Thad William
Foreman   Manes   **Walker**
1881-1923   1889-1974   1874-1952

Clara Mae Keener
1901-1957
= Benjamin F. **Lipscomb**
1897-1961

Willie Sue Keener
1905-1984
= A. Linder **Lipscomb**
1904-1969

- Eugene 1907-1995
  = Ruby ____
- Cornelia Elizabeth
  1909-1948
  = William V. Adams
- Esther Mae 1910-1999
  = Woodson "Pete" Martin Lawson
- Samuel Fred
  1911-1971
  = Rosa Lee Biddle
- Myrtle 1913-1997
  = Fred Scarborough
- Charles E. 1921-1970
  = Willie Mae Freeman
- Gladys E. 1922-2006
  = Paul E. Skidmore

- Bonnie L.
  1931-2014
  = James L. Pike
- Mary Frances
  1933-1985
  = Jan Lyons

- John Thomas
  1922-1922
- Delma Martin
  ca.1923-1965
- Ann Lipscomb
  1929-1929

- Doris Sue
  1926-(bef. 2010)
  = John Lawder
- Douglas Graves
  1928-1986
  = Katherine Frost

Manes–Foreman–Walker Family Tree[306]

MARTHA MASHBURN'S UNUSUAL FAMILY

Martha Mashburn Maness' early life was a puzzle to work out because of the maiden name passed down in her family, and her final years are still a puzzle. She was still living in 1910, in Mineral Spring, Moore County, with her widowed daughter Annie Morgan and one of Annie's children. One of Martha's daughters had predeceased her, possibly Fannie Mashburn (or Jones). Susan, who married John Thompson, might have been living as a servant in the Stutts household in Bensalem Township, Moore County in 1910.[307]

Martha's youngest, Fannie, might have been taken in by her uncle, Christopher Jones. However, the two Fannies have different birthdays and, with fifteen siblings, Chris could have taken in a niece by the same name from another part of the family. Fannie Mashburn disappears from all records after 1880, leaving only Fannie Jones.[308]

Annie remarried and lived until 1964. No death records have been found for her mother or sisters. Although there are several Martha Manesses buried in Moore County, none of them quite match up with Thomas' sixth wife.[309]

THE SEARCH FOR THOMAS MANESS

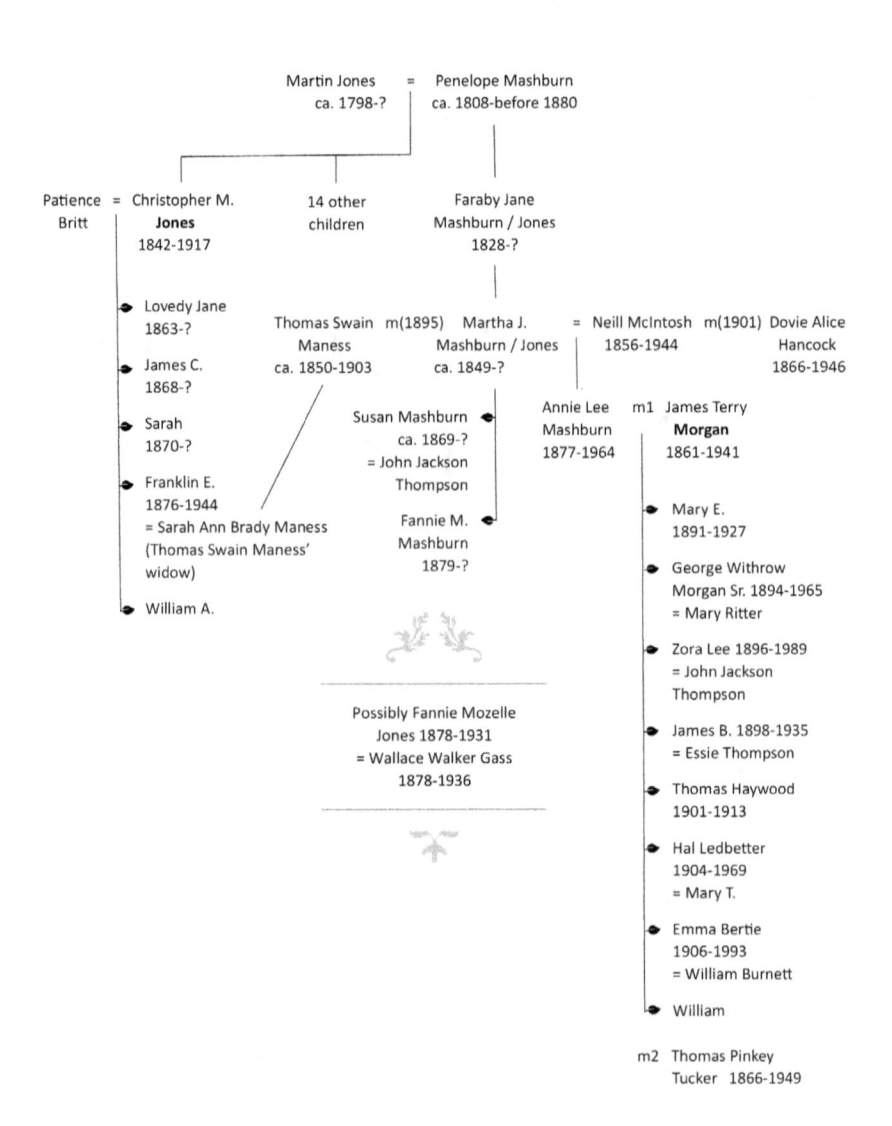

```
                    Martin Jones     =    Penelope Mashburn
                    ca. 1798-?            ca. 1808-before 1880
```

- Patience = Christopher M. Jones 1842-1917
- 14 other children
- Faraby Jane Mashburn / Jones 1828-?

- Lovedy Jane 1863-?
- James C. 1868-?
- Sarah 1870-?
- Franklin E. 1876-1944
  = Sarah Ann Brady Maness (Thomas Swain Maness' widow)
- William A.

Thomas Swain Maness ca. 1850-1903   m(1895)   Martha J. Mashburn / Jones ca. 1849-?   =   Neill McIntosh 1856-1944   m(1901)   Dovie Alice Hancock 1866-1946

- Susan Mashburn ca. 1869-? = John Jackson Thompson
- Fannie M. Mashburn 1879-?

Annie Lee Mashburn 1877-1964   m1   James Terry **Morgan** 1861-1941

- Mary E. 1891-1927
- George Withrow Morgan Sr. 1894-1965 = Mary Ritter
- Zora Lee 1896-1989 = John Jackson Thompson
- James B. 1898-1935 = Essie Thompson
- Thomas Haywood 1901-1913
- Hal Ledbetter 1904-1969 = Mary T.
- Emma Bertie 1906-1993 = William Burnett
- William

m2 Thomas Pinkey Tucker 1866-1949

Possibly Fannie Mozelle Jones 1878-1931 = Wallace Walker Gass 1878-1936

Mashburn-Jones Family Tree (abbreviated)[309b]

THE MANESS-JONES FAMILY

S ARAH BRADY MANESS HAD ONE ADVANTAGE over Thomas' other wives – she knew for certain he was dead.

Sarah was still young and had two small daughters to care for, although their birth records are confusing. Several records have Oppie born exactly three months after Cora. One social-security record shows Oppie born in June 1904, which makes more sense. Since Thomas Maness died in December 1903, he could still have been her father. DNA from descendants verifies that Cora was definitely his child.[310]

Sarah remarried, to Frank Jones in 1908. Sarah Brady and Martha Mashburn might have found out about each other after Thomas' death — Frank Jones was Martha's first cousin! Sarah and Frank had five more children: Lizzie, Lilly, Lloyd, a boy who died as an infant, and Charlie Garland Jones.[311] Sarah lived into 1964, passing away at age 86.[312]

Cora and Oppie Maness stayed in North Carolina, married and had families. Cora and Herbert Mitchell Brown had six children, including the three daughters mentioned earlier who outlived their mother: Lessie, Myrtle, and Lottie. At her death in 1994, Cora also had fifteen grandchildren and fourteen great-grandchildren. Lessie stayed in the Raleigh area, but her sisters moved to other states.[313] Oppie and James Edgar Chambers lived in Person County, N.C. and had four children: Lucille, Gertrude, Herman, and Minnie Marie. When Oppie died in 1986, she had sixteen grandchildren and twenty-four great-grandchildren.[314]

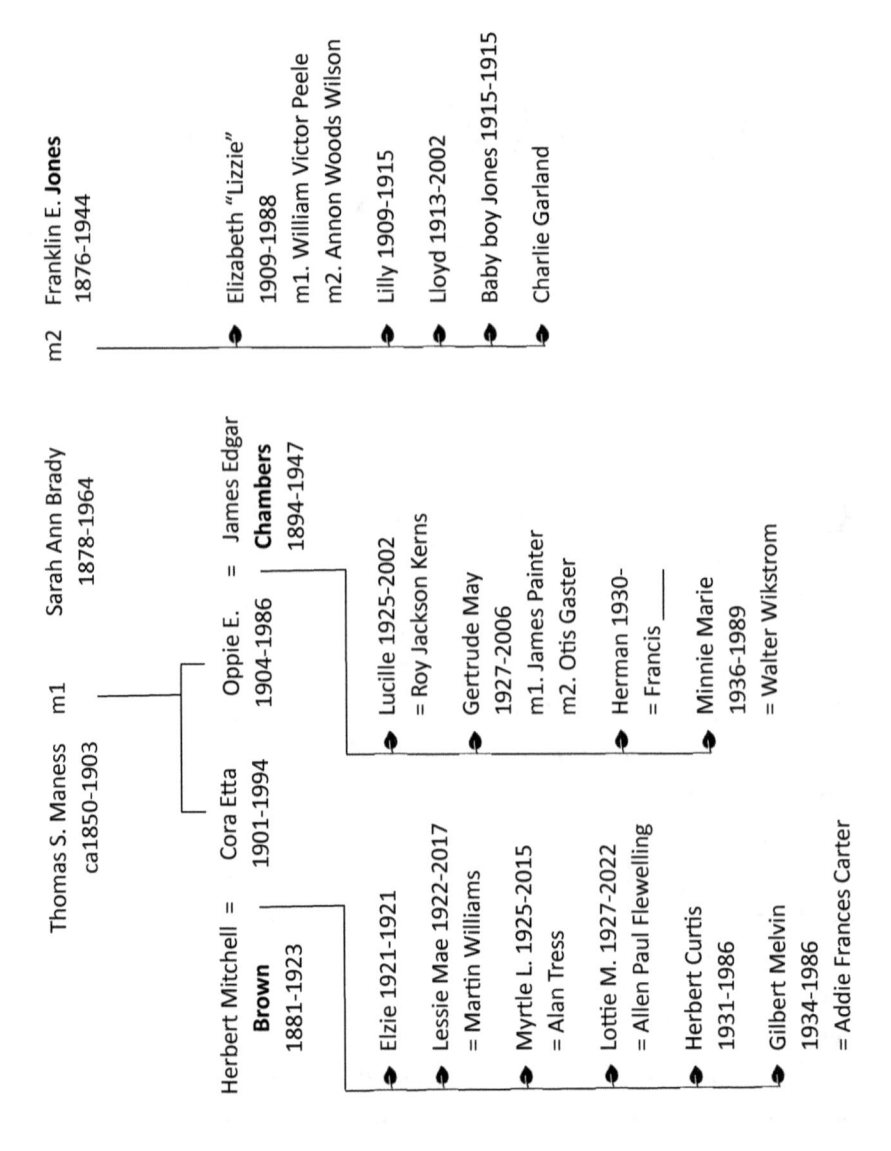

Maness-Jones Family Tree[315]

EPILOGUE

Finding out who Thomas was and what happened to him was a lifelong dream come true, and an answered prayer. The answer came with a long list of new questions. Who were Thomas' real parents? Was he truly one of the six siblings with the rhyming names? He's mysteriously absent from every census except for 1870, with his first wife. Whatever happened to his sisters?

I found more clues on a trip to Raleigh in 2013. Scrolling through dark microfilm, I found the Moore County marriage license for Thomas S. Maness and Martha Mashburn. It listed his age as 45, confirmation of his younger birth date (ca. 1850), which matched up with his age at Pandora's marriage. As I'd hoped, Thomas had given the names of his parents — neither the George Maness nor the Henry Maness I'd expected. His parents were George Hunsucker and Polly Maness.

There were three George Hunsuckers in upper Moore County in 1850, all related, all theoretically with the same Y-DNA. The abundant Mary "Polly" Manesses haven't been as easy to narrow down. The names still reveal an important insight. We didn't seem related to the Moore County Manesses through Y-DNA because we're not related to them through Thomas' *father*; we're related through his *mother*. Indeed, Thurman Maness eventually appeared as a distant cousin in the Family Finder matches.

Searching for more about Thomas will probably be a life-long journey (to continue that journey, join at elizabethasaunders.com). Like other genealogists who perpetually bemoan the loss of the 1890 census, I thought Thomas had dropped off the written records for nearly two decades (1876-1895, between his marriages to Nancy and Martha). As I was finishing the draft of this book, however, I discovered *two more wives* and families! I had to add the "Traveling Man" chapter (originally titled "The Missing Years") with Louisa Kelly and Willie Stewart.

Our family has called Thomas Maness a rascal, scoundrel, carpetbagger, black sheep. We laugh about it. I've "lived" with Thomas Maness as a progenitor of my family for more than 30 years now. His life wasn't funny. He caused a lot of sadness. He endured a lot of sadness. Pandora must have been broken-hearted when he never came home. His other wives must have felt the same grief.

Thurman Maness recalled his father — who knew Thomas firsthand — saying that Thomas was a nice boy before he went to war, but he came back kinda mean. As I uncovered the truth about Thomas' real age, that he was so much younger than anybody thought because of the misleading records, and the truth about his illegitimate parentage, I started to realize what an incredibly hard life he had. While I sympathize with his wives' grief of not knowing what happened to him and of feeling deserted, I can only theorize that Thomas had post-traumatic stress disorder from the war, combined with such an unstable childhood that he didn't even have the basic education to write his own name.

The women left behind worked hard to provide for their children, who prospered more with each generation. The pains have diminished through death, new generations, and the healing of nearly a century and a half. I can easily imagine Thomas as scrappy, a Tom Sawyer who didn't always obey the rules. I have a harder time imagining him as a Casanova, charming and seducing young women. Now we almost brag about Thomas as our black sheep, such a vivid character that he was.

We tell his stories. And we laugh. Because there's one truth we all know: if Thomas had behaved, if he'd bravely stood up to losing battles, if he'd stayed home and never gone philandering, we wouldn't be here.

ACKNOWLEDGEMENTS

THIS BOOK WOULD NOT HAVE BEEN possible without the work of other genealogists, including Lacy Garner, Thurman Maness, Morgan Jackson, and Don McCaskill. Debbie Hightower, Rausie Hobson, Sarah Katreen Hoggatt, and Joan Poole helped put this daunting project in much better shape. Any errors are mine, especially genealogical fact-checking, which never ends. Special thanks to family and friends who encouraged me and listened to every new discovery, especially my dear husband, Chris Johnson.

Appendix (Spoilers!)

Thomas S. Maness' Birth Date

Secondary sources, including written oral history, set Thomas as older than depicted in this narrative. Several written sources corroborate his birth date as ca. 1845-1850. I concluded that Thomas lied about his age to get into the military and then for his first marriage, making himself appear older in early records. His age (birth year) was more consistent throughout his later life, when he was no longer a minor.

There is a possible census record of Thomas in 1850, with the surname Campbell. Intriguingly, the head of the household is Mary Campbell and the siblings are Lundy, Leander, Alexander, Shadrach, and Mary C. Campbell. They were enumerated four houses from a George Hunsucker and family. If Thomas Maness were actually Sween Campbell, he would have been around 21 at enlistment, with no need to say he was 18. None of the other primary sources match such an early birth date. It's possible that this was actually his Maness family, and that the oldest child died and Thomas was born after the census enumeration. If Thomas were the oldest child instead of the youngest, the narrative of this story would change slightly. However, the war would still have had a traumatic effect on him.

Date of Record	Record	Birth Date
December 1956	Thomas Swain Maness' tombstone, based on George W. Wilcox and T.D. [Thurman] Maness' veteran headstone application, birth "about 1833"	1833
8 Nov. 1850	1850 U.S. Federal Census: Sween CAMPBELL, age 10; with mother Mary Campbell and siblings Lundy, Leander, Alexander, Shadrach, and Mary C.	11/9/1839-11/8/1840
After 1862	Compiled service record "Roll of Honor" for Tho's S. Maness, age 18 on enlistment, 13 June 1861	6/14/1842-6/13/1843
5 Sept. 186[6]	Maness-Craton marriage license, no age given	—
22 July 1870	1870 U.S Federal Census, age 25	7/23/1844-7/22/1845
19 June 1874	Maness-Wall marriage license, age 25	6/20/1848-6/19/1849
8 Dec. 1876	Maness-Pool marriage license, age 26	12/9/1849-12/8/1850
8 Dec. 1880	Maness-Kelly marriage license, age 35	12/9/1844-12/8/1845
28 April 1888	Maness-Stewart marriage license, no age given for Thomas	—
5 Oct. 1895	Maness-Mashburn marriage license, age 45	10/6/1849-10/5/1850
13 Dec. 1901	Maness-Brady marriage license, age 49	12/14/1851-12/13/1852

Bibliography

Publications

"Anniversary of Gettysburg, Forty Years After the Battle," *Charlotte Daily Observer*, Saturday Morning, July 4, 1903, http://www.26nc.org/Articles/Charlotte%20Daily%20Observer-articleedited.pdf, viewed July 21, 2019.

Beitzell, Edwin W., *Point Lookout Prison Camp for Confederates.* Leonardtown, Md.: St. Mary's County Historical Society, 1983, sixth printing, 2007.

Burgwyn, William H. S., edited by Herbert M. Schiller. *A Captain's War: The Letters and Diaries of William H. S. Burgwyn, 1861-1865.* Shippensburg, Penn.: White Mane Publishing Company, Inc., 1994.

Calkins, Chris. *Auto Tour of Civil War Petersburg, 1861-1865.* City of Petersburg, Virginia, 2003.

"Casualties in N. C. Troops," *Fayetteville Observer*, July 7, 1864, Vol. XIV, No. 1347. Fayetteville, N.C., 3.

"Casualties in N. C. Troops," *The North-Carolina Standard* (Weekly Standard), July 13, 1864, Vol. XXX, No. 18. Raleigh, 2.

Coltrane, Kay Davis. *Centre Friends: The Legacy of the Meeting on the Hill.* Greensboro: Centre Friends Meeting, 2008.

Davis, Jefferson, "Andersonville and Other War Prisons," *Confederate Veteran*, April 1907, Vol. XV, No. 4. Nashville, 163-164.

Davis, T. C. [No article title] *Confederate Veteran*, February 1899, Vol. VII, No. 2. Nashville, 65.

Day, W. A. *A True History of Company I, 49th Regiment, North Carolina Troops, in the Great Civil War, Between the North and South.* Newton, N.C., 1893.

"Editors Confederate," *The Daily Confederate*, July 8, 1864. Raleigh. Accessed via Library of Congress, chroniclingamerica.loc.gov, April 25, 2020, 2.

Eggleston, George Cary. *Southern Soldier Stories*, New York: Macmillan, 1898.

Ellis, F. P. [Peter]. "Wounded Boy's Night on a Battlefield," *Confederate Veteran* vol. XVII, No. 9, September 1909. Nashville – reprinted Wendell, N.C.: Broadfoot's Bookmark, 456.

Everton, George B. Jr. and Louise Mathews Everton. *The Handy Book for Genealogists, United States of America.* Logan, Utah: The Everton Publishers, Inc., eighth edition, 1991.

Gaddy, Capt. R. B. "White's Store," *The Messenger and Intelligencer*, Dec. 13, 1888. Wadesboro, N.C., 3.

Garner, Lacy. 26th Regiment N.C. State Troops, https://www.companyh26th.com/last-names-k-ma.html (viewed July 11, 2019 and other times, not available as of 2022).

Garner, Lacy A. Jr. *Tales from the Upper End of the County,* "Thurman Maness Remembers." Second edition, 2009.

Gragg, Rod. *Covered with Glory: The 26th North Carolina Infantry at the Battle of Gettysburg.* New York: Perennial – HarperCollins, 2000.

Graham, W. A. "Nineteenth Regiment (Second Cavalry)," Vol. II, *Histories of the Several Regiments and Battalions from North*

Carolina in the Great War 1861-'65, edited by Walter Clark. Goldsboro, N.C.: Nash Brothers [1901].

Haley, M. [Michael] J. "Report from an Andersonville Prisoner," *Confederate Veteran*, February 1907, Vol. XV, No. 2. Nashville, 57-58.

Holmes, Clay W. *Elmira Prison Camp: A History of the Military Prison at Elmira, N.Y., July 6, 1864, to July 10, 1865.* New York and London: G.P. Putnam's Sons, 1912.

Hughes, Fred. *Guilford County, North Carolina Historical Documentation* map, revised August 1988.

"In the Trenches at Petersburg," *The Confederate Veteran*, January 1926, Vol. XXXIV, No. 1. Nashville.

Jordan, Weymouth T. Jr. *North Carolina Troops, 1831-1865, A Roster*, Vol. XII Infantry, 49th-52nd Regiments. Raleigh: North Carolina Division of Archives and History, 1990.

Kennedy, Frances H., editor. *The Civil War Battlefield Guide*. Boston: Houghton Mifflin Co., 1990.

Kerr, Richard E. Jr. *Wall of Fire – The Rifle and Civil War Infantry Tactics*. M.S. thesis, Fort Leavenworth, Kansas: U.S. Army Command and General Staff College, 1990. http://www.dtic.mil/dtic/tr/fulltext/u2/a227467.pdf.

Krick, Robert E. L. "Malvern Hill: Portrait of a Battlefield," *Civil War: The Official Magazine of the Civil War Society*, no. 73, April 1999, especially map by Michael Gorman.

Leon, L. *Diary of a Tar Heel Confederate Soldier*. Charlotte: Stone Publishing, 1913.

McCaskill, Don. *Maness Families*. Biscoe, N.C., 2002.

McRae, D. K. and A. M. Gorman, editors. "From Virginia," *The Daily Confederate,* June 27, 1864. Raleigh. Accessed via Library of Congress, chroniclingamerica.loc.gov, May 12, 2020, 2.

Manarin, Louis H. *North Carolina Troops, 1861-1865, A Roster,* Vol. II, Cavalry. Raleigh, N.C.: State Division of Archives and History, second printing with addenda, 1989.

Manarin, Louis H. "26th Regiment N.C. Troops." In *North Carolina Troops, 1861-1865, A Roster,* Vol. VII, Infantry, 22nd-26th Regiments, compiled by Weymouth T. Jordan Jr. Raleigh: Division of Archives and History, 1979.

Manarin, Louis H. "43rd Regiment N.C. Troops." In *North Carolina Troops, 1861-1865, A Roster,* Vol. X, Infantry, 38th-39th And 42nd-44th Regiments, compiled by Weymouth T. Jordan Jr. Raleigh: Division of Archives and History, 1985.

Medley, Mary L. *History of Anson County, North Carolina, 1750-1976.* Wadesboro, N.C.: Anson County Historical Society, 1976.

Miller, William J. "Prelude: Eight Days to Decision," *Civil War: The Official Magazine of the Civil War Society,* no. 73, April 1999.

Moore County Heritage, North Carolina, Vol. I. Moore County Heritage Book Committee, 2005.

Opie, John N. *A Rebel Cavalryman with Lee, Stuart and Jackson.* Chicago: W. B. Conkey Company, 1899.

Phillips, Lois Smith and Carol Smith Purvis. *The Brady Family of Moore and Chatham Counties.* Charlotte: Herb Eaton Historical Publications, 1987.

Roulhac, Thomas R. *Forty-Ninth Regiment*, Vol. III, *Histories of the Several Regiments and Battalions from North Carolina in the Great War 1861-'65*, edited by Walter Clark. Goldsboro, N.C.: State of North Carolina, 1901.

Saunders, Elizabeth A. *Archdale Friends Meeting: Genealogical Extracts from the Monthly Meeting Minutes: 1924-1949.* Baltimore: Gateway Press, 2005.

Sneden, Robert Knox. *Plan of the Battle of Newberne North Carolina, Fought March 14th 1862* [map ca. 1862-1865]. Retrieved from the Library of Congress, https://www.loc.gov/item/gvhs01.vhs00079/. (Accessed September 24, 2016.)

"Southern Items," *Economist Falcon* (*The Weekly Economist*), May 26, 1891. Elizabeth City, N.C., 1.

"State and General News," *The Dispatch*, July 28, 1892. Lexington, N.C., 2.

Stepp, J. H. "Determined Tenacity: The 26th Regiment North Carolina Troops at Gettysburg," *Company Front*, no. 2, 2008. The Society for the Preservation of the 26th Regiment North Carolina Troops, Inc., http://www.26nc.org/Company-Front/Archive/2008/Company_Front_Issue_2_2008.pdf.

Stokes, Durward T. *Company Shops: The Town Built by a Railroad.* Winston-Salem, N.C.: John F. Blair, 1981.

Triebe, Richard H. *Fort Fisher to Elmira: The Fatal Journey of 518 Confederate Soldiers.* Coastal Books, 2013.

Underwood, George C. *Twenty-Sixth Regiment*, Vol. II, *Histories of the Several Regiments and Battalions from North Carolina in the Great War 1861-'65*, edited by Walter Clark. Goldsboro, N.C.: State of North Carolina, 1901.

L. C. Vass (writing from Salem, Va. on 12 May 1890), "Jottings From Salem, Va." *New Berne Weekly Journal,* May 22, 1890. New Bern, N.C., 3.

Wakeman, Rosetta, edited by Lauren Cook Burgess. *An Uncommon Soldier: The Civil War Letters of Sarah Rosetta Wakeman, alias Private Lyons Wakeman, 153rd Regiment, New York State Volunteers.* Pasadena, Md.: The Minerva Center, 1994.

Manuscripts and Interviews

Burgwyn, Henry K. Jr. Letters to his father and mother, July 2, 1862. Burgwyn Family Papers #1687, Southern Historical Collection, Wilson Library, University of North Carolina at Chapel Hill.

Compiled Service Records of Confederate Soldiers Who Served in Organizations from the State of North Carolina, National Archives M270, Record Group 109.

Deed from Martha Chappell to Pandora Maness in Sumner Township, dated March 22, 1899. Guilford County Register of Deeds, Book 117, 798-799.

Deed from Thomas Gossett Sr. to Thomas Gossett Jr. for 126 acres on Deep River, dated November 14, 1812. Guilford County Register of Deeds, Book 11, 58-59.

Deed from Samuel Stanton Sr. of Randolph County to Thomas Gossett Jr. for 212 acres on Deep River, dated March 21, 1815. Book 12, 41-42, Guilford County Register of Deeds.

Garner, Lacy, interview by the author, July 24, 2010.

Gordon, Gail, interview by the author, May 6, 2017.

Gordon, Linda Gail. "'Taylor' Family Record as of Late 1700's," 2017.

Maners, Martin A. Jr., interview by the author, April 24, 2021.

Maness, Dorcas Rebecca "Beth," interview by the author, April 8, 2023.

Maness, Thurman, interview by the author, March 7, 2008.

"Mrs. Agnes Manes et als vs. C. P. Sifford et als," Chancery files, 1924-1932. Circuit Court of Pulaski County, Virginia.

Muster Rolls, Company H, 26th Regiment, June 30, 1862 to June 30, 1863. Raleigh: North Carolina Archives, Civil War Collection, Box 52.1.

Richardson, A. M. *Map of the Southern Express Company.* Charleston, S.C.: Walker, Evans & Cogswell, Engravers, 1884, Library of Congress.

Skidmore, Mark, interview by the author, April 21, 2022.

Notes

1. Thomas S. Maness' military records, *Compiled Service Records of Confederate Soldiers Who Served in Organizations from the State of North Carolina*, National Archives M270, Record Group 109, accessed via Fold3.

2. See the appendix, Thomas S. Maness' birth date.

3. Durward T. Stokes, *Company Shops: The Town Built by a Railroad* (Winston-Salem, N.C.: John F. Blair, 1981), 1-16.

4. George C. Underwood, *Twenty-Sixth Regiment*, Vol. II, *Histories of the Several Regiments and Battalions from North Carolina in the Great War 1861-'65*, edited by Walter Clark (Goldsboro, N.C.: State of North Carolina, 1901), 303-305.

5. Ibid., 305-306.

6. Rod Gragg, *Covered with Glory: The 26th North Carolina Infantry at the Battle of Gettysburg* (New York: Perennial – HarperCollins, 2000), 10.

7. Rosetta Wakeman, edited by Lauren Cook Burgess, *An Uncommon Soldier: The Civil War Letters of Sarah Rosetta Wakeman, alias Private Lyons Wakeman, 153rd Regiment, New York State Volunteers* (Pasadena, Md.: The Minerva Center, 1994), 31.

8. Gragg, 12.

9. Gragg, 13. General description of Bogue Banks from Wikipedia and http://www.carteretcountync.gov/297/History-of-Bogue-Banks, accessed May 19, 2017.

10. Underwood, 307.

11. Richard E. Kerr Jr., *Wall of Fire – The Rifle and Civil War Infantry Tactics* (M.S. thesis, Fort Leavenworth, Kansas: U.S. Army Command and General Staff College, 1990), 29-33, http://www.dtic.mil/dtic/tr/fulltext/u2/a227467.pdf.

[12] Underwood, 307.

[13] Underwood, 307-308; Louis H. Manarin, "26th Regiment N.C. Troops." In *North Carolina Troops, 1861-1865, A Roster*, Vol. VII, Infantry, compiled by Weymouth T. Jordan Jr. (Raleigh: Division of Archives and History, 1979), 455.

[14] Maness Family Collection. Privately held by Elizabeth A. Saunders, Archdale, N.C.

[15] Manarin, *NC Troops*, Vol. VII, Infantry, 455; Underwood, 307-308; Gragg, 19.

[16] Alexander Maness' military records, *Compiled Service Records of Confederate Soldiers Who Served in Organizations from the State of North Carolina*, National Archives M270, Record Group 109, accessed via Fold3.

[17] Louis H. Manarin, *North Carolina Troops, 1861-1865, A Roster*, Vol. II, Cavalry (Raleigh, N.C.: State Division of Archives and History, second printing with addenda, 1989), 98.

[18] W. A. Graham, "Nineteenth Regiment (Second Cavalry)," Vol. II, *Histories of the Several Regiments and Battalions from North Carolina in the Great War 1861-'65,* edited by Walter Clark (Goldsboro, N.C.: Nash Brothers [1901]), 81-82.

[19] Robert Knox Sneden, *Plan of the Battle of Newberne North Carolina, Fought March 14th 1862* [map ca 1862-1865]. Library of Congress, https://www.loc.gov/item/gvhs01.vhs00079/; Underwood, 308-309.

[20] Underwood, 310, 329.

[21] Related by Capt. Thomas J. Cureton in Underwood, 328-329.

[22] Underwood, 309-322.

[23] Ibid., facing 309.

[24] Ibid., 322-325.

[25] 1880 census, Sumner Township, Guilford County, N.C.

Notes

26 Maness-Wall marriage license, Sumner Township, Guilford County, N.C., June 25, 1874.

27 Graham, 81; Underwood, 322-324.

28 Underwood, 322-329.

29 Ibid.; Gragg, 21.

30 Underwood, 303.

31 Ibid.

32 Graham, 79.

33 Underwood, 323.

34 Ibid., 322-326.

35 Manarin, *NC Troops,* Vol. VII, Infantry, 456.

36 Underwood, 327-328.

37 Ibid., 328-330.

38 Ibid., 327-328; Thomas S. Maness' military records.

39 Gragg, 21.

40 Underwood, 331.

41 Gragg, 24-25.

42 Ira L. Maness' military records, *Compiled Service Records of Confederate Soldiers Who Served in Organizations from the State of North Carolina,* National Archives M270, Record Group 109, accessed via Fold3; Manarin, *NC Troops,* Vol. VII, Infantry, 568.

43 Underwood, 331-332.

44 Manarin, *NC Troops,* Vol. VII, Infantry, 457.

45 Underwood, 332.

46 Manarin, *NC Troops,* Vol. VII, Infantry, 457; William J. Miller, "Prelude: Eight Days to Decision," *Civil War: The Official Magazine of the Civil War Society,* no. 73, April 1999. — The fact that the Twenty-sixth arrived at the beginning, not towards the end of

the Seven Days Campaign, plus the map with dates (no author), helped with overall concepts of the battle of Malvern Hill.

47 Robert E. L. Krick, "Malvern Hill: Portrait of a Battlefield," *Civil War: The Official Magazine of the Civil War Society*, no. 73, April 1999, especially maps by Michael Gorman.

48 Underwood, 332.

49 Henry K. Burgwyn Jr. to his father and mother, July 2, 1862, Burgwyn Family Papers #1687, Chapel Hill: Southern Historical Collection, Wilson Library, University of North Carolina.

50 Robert Knox Sneden, *Plan of the Battle of Malvern Hill, Virginia. Fought June 30th and July 1st* [1862-1865], Geography and Map Division, Library of Congress [Virginia Historical Society], https://www.loc.gov/item/gvhs01.vhs00252/.

51 Underwood, 331-333.

52 Gragg, 27-28; Burgwyn letters.

53 Burgwyn letters.

54 Gragg, 28.

55 Underwood, 331-333.

56 F. P. Ellis, "Wounded Boy's Night on a Battlefield," *Confederate Veteran*, vol. XVII, No. 9, September 1909 (Nashville – reprinted Wendell, N.C.: Broadfoot's Bookmark), 456; Name of author as Peter, matching age and Thirteenth Mississippi, Company I from U.S., Civil War Soldier Records and Profiles, 1861-1865, accessed via Ancestry.com Jan. 1, 2021.

57 Gragg, 29; Burgwyn letters.

58 Burgwyn letters.

59 Underwood, 333; Ellis, 456.

60 Frances H. Kennedy, ed., *The Civil War Battlefield Guide*. (Boston: Houghton Mifflin Co., 1990).

61 Garner, Lacy. 26th Regiment N.C. State Troops, https://www.companyh26th.com/last-names-k-ma.html (viewed July 11, 2019

and other times, not available as of 2022, hereafter referenced as Garner, Company H); Ira L. Maness' military records; Manarin, *NC Troops*, Vol. VII, Infantry, 568.

62 Underwood, 400-401.

63 Ibid., 334-36; Manarin, *NC Troops*, vol. VII, Infantry, 457.

64 Underwood, 340.

65 Ibid., 339-341; Gragg, 36.

66 J. H. Stepp, "Determined Tenacity: The 26th Regiment North Carolina Troops at Gettysburg," *Company Front*, 2008, no. 2 (The Society for the Preservation of the 26th Regiment North Carolina Troops, Inc.), http://www.26nc.org/Company-Front/Archive/2008/Company_Front_Issue_2_2008.pdf, viewed July 31, 2019, 22-23.

67 1860 census, Gold Region, Moore County, N.C.; 1860 Moore Co. slave schedules.

68 Shadrach Maness' military records, *Compiled Service Records of Confederate Soldiers Who Served in Organizations from the State of North Carolina*, National Archives M270, Record Group 109, accessed via Fold3; Lacy A. Garner, Jr., *Tales from the Upper End of the County, "Thurman Maness Remembers"* (second edition, 2009, hereafter referenced as Garner, *Tales*), 182-188; Weymouth T. Jordan Jr., *North Carolina Troops, 1831-1865, A Roster*, Vol. XII, Infantry, 49th-52nd Regiments (Raleigh: North Carolina Division of Archives and History, 1990). Conscription Act with ages and fine mentioned in *An Account of the Sufferings of Friends Of North Carolina Yearly Meeting, in support of their Testimony against War, from 1861 to 1865*, NCYM, Seventh Month 18th, 1868.

69 Jordan, *NC Troops*, Vol. XII, Infantry, 8-9.

70 Shadrach Maness' military records; Jordan, *NC Troops*, Vol. XII, Infantry, 1.

71 Graham, 81-87.

72 Manarin, *NC Troops*, Vol. II, Cavalry, 99; George Cary Eggleston, *Southern Soldier Stories* (New York: Macmillan, 1898), 121.

73 Graham, 87; "Jeb" as a nickname in Eggleston, 121.

74 Graham, 81-82.

75 Manarin, *NC Troops*, Vol. II, Cavalry, 100.

76 Ibid.; Graham 87-88, 93.

77 Graham, 88-90.

78 Edwin Forbes, *Cavalry Charge Near Brandy Station, Virginia, 1864,* Morgan collection of Civil War drawings, Library of Congress Prints and Photographs Division, http://hdl.loc.gov/loc.pnp/cph.3a04943.

79 Graham, 88-93; Manarin, *NC Troops*, Vol. II, Cavalry, 101.

80 Alexander L. Maness' military records.

81 Ibid.; Manarin, *NC Troops*, Vol. II, Cavalry, 100-101, 168.

82 Gragg, 39.

83 Ibid., 44-45; Manarin, *NC Troops*, Vol. VII, Infantry, 459.

84 Underwood, 342; Gragg, 46-47.

85 Gragg, 65.

86 Underwood, 342; Alexander L. Maness' military records; Muster Roll, Company H of the 26th Regiment of N.C. Troops, May 1, 1863 to June 30, 1863, Raleigh, North Carolina Archives.

87 Underwood, 342-343.

88 Ibid., 343; Manarin, *NC Troops*, Vol. VII, Infantry, 459; Gragg, 81-88.

89 Underwood, 343; Manarin, *NC Troops*, Vol. VII, Infantry, 459.

90 Underwood, 343-349; Manarin, *NC Troops*, Vol. VII, Infantry, 459.

91 Underwood, 346-350.

92 Ibid., 350-351.

Notes 177

93 Ibid., 351-356, 383; Library of Congress video, "Rare Footage of Civil War Veterans Doing the Rebel Yell," https://www.youtube.com/watch?v=s6jSqt39vFM, viewed July 31, 2019.

94 Underwood, 351-352.

95 Stepp, *Company Front,* 23-25.

96 Underwood, 352; Stepp, *Company Front,* 25.

97 Underwood, 352.

98 Ibid., 353.

99 Ibid., 355; Manarin, *NC Troops,* Vol. VII, Infantry, 459-460.

100 Manarin, Vol. VII, Infantry, 460.

101 Col. William F. Fox, *Regimental Losses in the Civil War,* quoted in Underwood, 360.

102 "Anniversary of Gettysburg, Forty Years After the Battle," *Charlotte Daily Observer,* Saturday Morning, July 4, 1903, http://www.26nc.org/Articles/Charlotte%20Daily%20Observerarticleedited.pdf, viewed July 21, 2019.

103 Underwood, 366.

104 Beth Maness, "Sadberry Maness," *Moore County Heritage, North Carolina,* Vol. I (Moore County Heritage Book Committee, 2005), 212; Jonas S. Maness' military records, *Compiled Service Records of Confederate Soldiers Who Served in Organizations from the State of North Carolina,* National Archives M270, Record Group 109, accessed via Fold3; Manarin, *NC Troops,* Vol. VII, Infantry, 568.

105 John McGilvary's letter, in Garner, Company H; Manarin, *NC Troops,* Vol. VII, 562, 568; Bradley Brady's military records, *Compiled Service Records of Confederate Soldiers Who Served in Organizations from the State of North Carolina,* National Archives M270, Record Group 109, accessed via Fold3; Beth Maness, *Moore County Heritage,* 212; Jonas S. Maness' military records. Sedberry was hit during the first day but the exact moment or

part of the battle is unknown. Which day Bradley was wounded is unknown.

[106] Thomas S. Maness' military records; Manarin, *NC Troops*, Vol. VII, Infantry, 563-568; Muster Roll, Company H, May 1, 1863 to June 30, 1863; Garner, Company H.

[107] Chris Calkins, *Auto Tour of Civil War Petersburg, 1861-1865* (City of Petersburg, Virginia, 2003), 12.

[108] Muster Roll of Company H, 26th Regiment, June 30, 1862 to June 30, 1863. Raleigh, N.C.: North Carolina Archives, Civil War Collection, Box 52.1, 2017.

[109] Thurman Maness, interview by the author, March 7, 2008; Muster Rolls, Company H; Garner, *Tales*, 101.

[110] Calkins, 35.

[111] Underwood, 359, 372.

[112] Ibid., 370, 375-377.

[113] Ibid., 370-378.

[114] Thomas S. Maness' military records.

[115] Underwood, 378-379.

[116] Ibid., 380.

[117] Ibid., 380-381.

[118] Jonas S. Maness' military records; Bradley Brady's military records; Beth Maness, *Moore County Heritage*, 212; Manarin, *NC Troops*, Vol. VII, Infantry, 562.

[119] Thomas S. Maness' military records.

[120] Manarin, *NC Troops*, Vol. II, Cavalry, 101-102, 168.

[121] Alexander L. Maness' military records.

[122] Jones' quote related by an unnamed regiment soldier in Underwood, 382.

[123] Manarin, *NC Troops*, Vol. VII, Infantry, 461.

[124] Ibid., 461-462.

NOTES

125 Bradley Brady in Manarin, *NC Troops*, Vol. VII, Infantry, 562; Garner, Company H.

126 Thomas S. Maness' military records.

127 Ibid.

128 Ibid.; Edwin W. Beitzell, *Point Lookout Prison Camp for Confederates* (Leonardtown, Md.: St. Mary's County Historical Society, 1983, sixth printing 2007), 21-23, 76; Richard H. Triebe, *Fort Fisher to Elmira: The Fatal Journey of 518 Confederate Soldiers* (Coastal Books, 2013), 131.

129 Triebe, 105, 131; Beitzell, 76.

130 Beitzell, 76.

131 Triebe, 131.

132 Beitzell, 77.

133 Alexander L. Maness' military records.

134 William H. S. Burgwyn, edited by Herbert M. Schiller, *A Captain's War: The Letters and Diaries of William H. S. Burgwyn, 1861-1865* (Shippensburg, Penn.: White Mane Publishing Company, Inc., 1994), 154-160.

135 *Point Lookout, Md., View of Hammond Gen'l Hospital & U.S. Gen'l Depot for Prisoners of War*, Lith. by E. Sachse & Co., Baltimore (Point Lookout, Md.: George Everett, 1864). Library of Congress Geography and Map Division, https://lccn.loc.gov/99447401. Notations added.

136 Shadrach Maness' military records.

137 W. A. Day, *A True History of Company I, 49th Regiment, North Carolina Troops, in the Great Civil War, Between the North and South* (Newton, N.C.: 1893), 61-62; Jordan, Vol. XII, Infantry, 13.

138 Ibid.

139 Thomas R. Roulhac, *Forty-Ninth Regiment*, Vol. III, *Histories of the Several Regiments and Battalions from North Carolina in the*

Great War 1861-'65, edited by Walter Clark (Goldsboro, N.C.: State of North Carolina, 1901), 135-137.

[140] Ibid.

[141] Ibid., 137-139.

[142] Eggleston, 70-71.

[143] W. A. Day, quoted in "In the Trenches at Petersburg," *The Confederate Veteran,* Vol. XXXIV, No. 1 (Nashville, Tenn., January 1926), p. 23, accessed via archive.org May 2020; Jordan, *NC Troops*, Vol. XII, Infantry, 15.

[144] Jordan, *NC Troops*, Vol. XII, Infantry, 15.

[145] Eggleston, 72.

[146] Ibid., 232-233.

[147] Jordan, *NC Troops*, Vol. XII, Infantry, 15-16; "Day in the Trenches at Petersburg."

[148] Timothy H. O'Sullivan, *Blandford church, Petersburg, Va. April 1865,* April 1865. Civil war photographs, 1861-1865, Library of Congress Prints and Photographs Division, https://lccn.loc.gov/2018672391.

[149] Shadrach Maness' military records.

[150] Ed. D. K. McRae, A. M. Gorman, "From Virginia," *The Daily Confederate* (Raleigh, N.C.), June 27, 1864, 2, accessed via Library of Congress, chroniclingamerica.loc.gov, May 12, 2020.

[151] T. W. Dandridge quoted in "Editors Confederate," *The Daily Confederate*, July 8, 1864, accessed via chroniclingamerica.loc.gov, April 25, 2020, 2.

[152] "Casualties in N. C. Troops," *The North-Carolina Standard* (Weekly Standard), (Raleigh) July 13, 1864, Vol. XXX, No. 18, 2; "Casualties in N. C. Troops," *Fayetteville* (N.C.) *Observer*, July 7, 1864, Vol. XIV, No. 1347, 3.

[153] Garner, *Tales,* 188; Calkins, 36.

[154] Triebe, 132-133.

NOTES

[155] Thomas S. Maness' military records; Triebe, 113, 120, 143-147.

[156] Triebe, 143.

[157] Ibid., 154, 176, 185.

[158] Ibid., 120, 143, 176.

[159] Ibid., 108-110.

[160] Moulton & Larkin, *Elmira camp for Confederate prisoners with tents*, 1864, Library of Congress Prints and Photographs Division, https://lccn.loc.gov/2012647765.

[161] Triebe, 114-115, 135, 144, 160-161, 185; John N. Opie, *A Rebel Cavalryman with Lee, Stuart and Jackson* (Chicago: W. B. Conkey Company, 1899), accessed via Google books, May 2020, 319; T. C. Davis, *Confederate Veteran* (Nashville), February 1899, Vol. VII, No. 2 [No article title; he's from a North Carolina Regiment.], 65.

[162] Triebe, 110-115, 162; John I. Van Allen, quoted in Jefferson Davis, "Andersonville and Other War Prisons," *Confederate Veteran*, April 1907, Vol. XV, No. 4, 163-164.

[163] M. [Michael] J. Haley, "Report from an Andersonville Prisoner," *Confederate Veteran*, February 1907, Vol. XV, No. 2, 57-58.

[164] Ibid., 58; Triebe 115-118, 135, 146, 185.

[165] Triebe 108-109, 118-120, 125, 133 185.

[166] Ibid., 145.

[167] Ibid., 120-121, 147-148, 173, 194; Van Allen, *Confederate Veteran*, 164.

[168] Triebe, 144, 159; Davis, *Confederate Veteran*, 65.

[169] Opie, 318; Triebe, 120.

[170] Triebe, 147.

[171] Thomas S. Maness' military records.

[172] Triebe, 148.

[173] L. Leon, *Diary of a Tar Heel Confederate Soldier* (Charlotte: Stone Publishing, 1913), 68.

[174] Triebe, 139, 148, 154; Davis, 65.

[175] Triebe, 148-149.

[176] Ibid., 125.

[177] Ibid., 155, 165-166; Clay W. Holmes, *Elmira Prison Camp: A History of the Military Prison at Elmira, N.Y., July 6, 1864, to July 10, 1865* (New York and London: G.P. Putnam's Sons, 1912), 123-125. Accounts in Triebe say the flood rose up to six feet, while Holmes states the flood rose from six inches to two feet inside the barracks. Holmes later says that this flood was at least three feet higher at the high mark than the flood of 1889.

[178] Triebe, 150, 166; Holmes, 123-125.

[179] Holmes, 255; Triebe, 129.

[180] Thomas S. Maness' military records; Triebe, 167-168; Davis, 65.

[181] Triebe, 133, 138, 167-168.

[182] Thomas S. Maness' military records.

[183] Ibid.

[184] Burgwyn, *A Captain's War*, 175-176; Alexander Maness' military records.

[185] Thurman Maness interview, 2008; Calkins, 36.

[186] Thurman Maness interview, 2008; *Moore County Heritage*, 211-212; Don McCaskill, *Maness Families* (Biscoe, N.C.), 17; Reuben Maness' military records, *Compiled Service Records of Confederate Soldiers Who Served in Organizations from the State of North Carolina*, National Archives M270, Record Group 109, accessed via Fold3. Reuben died August 11, 1864.

[187] Garner, *Tales*, 188; Shadrach Maness' tombstone, Pleasant Hill United Methodist Cemetery (Robbins, N.C.), visited by the author in 2015.

[188] 1870 Federal Census, Bensalem Township, Moore County, enumerated July 18, 1870.

NOTES

[189] 1870 Federal Census, Bensalem Township, Moore County, enumerated July 25, 1870.

[190] 1870 Federal Census, Bensalem Township, Moore County, enumerated July 16, 1870.

[191] Hugh A. Maness' death certificate, North Carolina, Death Certificates, 1909-1975.

[192] Maness-Craton marriage license, Chatham County, N.C., Sept. 5, 1866.

[193] 1870 Federal Census, Chatham County, N.C., enumerated July 22, 1870.

[194] Elizabeth A. Saunders, "Simplified Map of Moore County," based on Jna. McDuffie and J. L. Currie, *Township Map of Moore County, N. C., 1886* (Edward W. Shedd), Moore County Public Library, Carthage, N.C.

[195] Ibid.; 1880 Federal Census, Chatham County, N.C., enumerated June --- 1880; William Nuton Maynor's and Bob Maynor's death certificates, North Carolina, U.S. Death Certificates, 1909-1976, 1926 and 1952.

[196] 1870 Federal Census, Sumner Township, Guilford County, enumerated Aug. 24, 1870; Fred Hughes, *Guilford County, North Carolina Historical Documentation* map, revised August 1988; Guilford County, N.C., Book 12: 41-42, deed from Samuel Stanton Sr. of Randolph County to Thomas Gossett Jr. for 212 acres on Deep River, March 21, 1815, Register of Deeds, Greensboro; 58-59, deed from Thomas Gossett Sr. to Thomas Gossett Jr. for 126 acres on Deep River, November 14, 1812; 798-799, deed from Martha Chappell to Pandora Maness in Sumner Township, March 22, 1899, references land deeded to Martha from her father, Thomas Gossett Jr; Johnson, William Perry Johnson, ed., *Tax List of Guilford Co., N.C.*, 1975.

[197] 1870 census, Sumner Township, Guilford County, N.C., enumerated Aug. 24, 1870; Kay Davis Coltrane, *Centre Friends: The*

Legacy of the Meeting on the Hill (Greensboro: Centre Friends Meeting, 2008), 56-67.

[198] Maness-Wall marriage license, Guilford County, N.C., June 25, 1874.

[199] 1870 census, Jonesboro, Mill Township, Indiana, enumerated July 20, 1870, and multiple other records for Jonathan Wiley Wall; Maness Family Collection with family oral history, specifically Oscar Maness' written notes from an undated interview with his grandmother, Emma Ellen English Maness.

[200] Frank Wiley Maness' death certificate, North Carolina, Death Certificates, 1909-1975; 1860 census, Saline County, Missouri (for Martha's sister Alice and husband Norwood Wiley).

[201] Mary Jane Chappell Waldon Priest's birth from her tombstone at Centre Friends Meeting, Guilford County, N.C.; 1880 census, Sumner Township, Guilford County, enumerated June 8, 1880; Family oral history.

[202] Frank Wiley Maness with unknown woman, photograph, ca. 1895; Maness Family Collection, privately held by Elizabeth A. Saunders. Collection passed down from Frank Wiley Maness to his son, Frank Vance Maness and family. The author recognizes that the woman is not his wife, whom he married in 1895; the photographer became active in the area in 1895 according to Stephen E. Massengill, *Photographers in North Carolina: The First Century, 1842-1941* (Raleigh: North Carolina Office of Archives and History, 2004), 124.

[203] L. C. Vass (writing from Salem, Va. on 12 May 1890), "Jottings From Salem, Va." *New Berne* (N.C.) *Weekly Journal*, May 22, 1890, 3.

[204] 1870 census, Blacksburg, Montgomery County, Virginia, enumerated Aug. 17, 1870.

[205] Maness-Pool marriage record, Giles County, Virginia, December 13, 1876, Virginia, Select Marriages, 1785-1940.

NOTES

206 Fannie Sifford death certificate, Dublin, Pulaski County, Virginia, 1921; Moses Pool in Virginia, Deaths and Burials Index, 1853-1917; 1880 census, Pembroke, Giles County, Virginia.

207 "Southern Items," *Economist Falcon (The Weekly Economist)* (Elizabeth City, N.C.) May 26, 1891, 1.

208 "State and General News," *The Dispatch*, (Lexington, N.C.) July 28, 1892, 2.

209 Thurman Maness' maternal grandfather was Presley Maness, Sedberry's brother and first cousin to Henry Maness, Thomas Swain Maness' supposed father. Thurman's paternal grandfather was Tommy P. Maness, mentioned in an earlier chapter.

210 Thurman Maness interview, 2008; also in Garner, *Tales*, 100-101.

211 Moore County courthouse, Carthage, N.C., photo in undated clipping (prior to the courthouse fire in 1889); Moore County Public Library, Carthage, N.C.

212 Thurman Maness interview, 2008; negative search of Moore County court records for Thomas Maness' arrest or any charges and case.

213 Mary L. Medley, *History of Anson County, North Carolina, 1750-1976* (Wadesboro, N.C., Anson County Historical Society, 1976), 118-123; Capt. R. B. Gaddy, "White's Store," *The Messenger and Intelligencer*, (Wadesboro, N.C.) Dec. 13, 1888, 3.

214 Louis H. Manarin, "43rd Regiment N.C. Troops." In *North Carolina Troops, 1861-1865, A Roster*, Vol. X, Infantry, compiled by Weymouth T. Jordan Jr. (Raleigh: Division of Archives and History, 1985), 365; Louisa Kelly's birth date from her death certificate, Gaston County, N.C., 1930, in North Carolina, U.S., Death Certificates, 1909-1976.

215 Maness-Kelly marriage license, Anson County, N.C., Dec. 12, 1880.

216 Richardson, A. M. *Map of the Southern Express Company* (Charleston, S.C., Walker, Evans & Cogswell, 1884). Library of Congress

Geography and Map Division, https://lccn.loc.gov/gm71000842. Notations added.

[217] Ibid.; 1880 census, Lanesboro Township, Anson County, N.C., enumerated June 7, 1880.

[218] 1900 census, Peachland and Polkton, Lanesboro Township, Anson County, N.C., enumerated June 7, 1900: Louisa was listed as a widow who had had six children, with four living.

[219] Thomas C. Manes' death certificate, Canonsburg, Washington Co., Penn., 1924.

[220] Herman Fantom Maners' death certificate, Guilford County, N.C., 1967, in North Carolina, U.S., Death Certificates, 1909-1976.

[221] Manes-Stewart marriage license, Etowah County, Alabama, April 29, 1888, 273, viewed Nov. 29, 2020, via Family Search; Cora's birth date from her tombstone, database, *Find a Grave* (https://www.findagrave.com/memorial/87290357/cora-elizabeth-foreman_walker, 2012), viewed May 6, 2022.

[222] A. M. Richardson, *Map of the Southern Express Company*.

[223] 1900 census, Peachland and Polkton, Lanesboro Township, Anson County, N.C.; William Harvey Maners' birth date in North Carolina, U.S., Birth Indexes, 1800-2000, Anson County, File no. D-7, 107; Frank Maners' birth date in his death certificate, Mecklenburg County, N.C., 1958.

[224] 1900 census, Peachland and Polkton, Lanesboro Township has Louisa as a widow; Maness-Mashburn marriage license, Bensalem, Moore County, N.C., Oct. 6, 1895.

[225] Unlabeled tintype photos; Maness Family Collection.

[226] Frank Wiley Maness, ca. 1890s; Maness Family Collection.

[227] Ibid. Original photograph is blurry.

[228] Garner, *Tales*, 100, 182-188.

[229] Garner, *Tales*, 102.

NOTES

[230] 1870 census, Carters Mills, Bensalem Township, Moore County, N.C., enumerated July 25, 1870.

[231] Ibid.; 1860 census, Gold Region, Moore County, N.C., enumerated Aug. 9, 1860; Martha's grandmother's name from Amariah Jones' death certificate, Moore County, N.C., 1923.

[232] 1880 census, Carthage Township, Moore County, N.C., enumerated June 25, 1880; Annie Mashburn marriage, 1930, in Virginia, Select Marriages 1785-1940; McIntosh-Hancock marriage in North Carolina, Marriage Records, 1741-2011, Dec. 24, 1901.

[233] Maness-Mashburn North Carolina marriage license, Moore County, 1895; North Carolina Marriage Index, 1741-2004.

[234] Ibid.

[235] Ibid.

[236] Lois Smith Phillips and Carol Smith Purvis, *The Brady Family of Moore and Chatham Counties* (Charlotte, Herb Eaton Historical Publications, 1987), 1-6, 2-7 to 2-9, 3-1 to 3-6, 4-24, 7-1, 7-12, 7-71 to 7-75.

[237] Cora Maness Brown's death certificate, North Carolina, Vital Records Section, 1994; Maness-Brady marriage license, Moore County, N.C., Dec. 13, 1901.

[238] Maness-Mashburn marriage license; 1900 census, Black Jack township, Richmond County, N.C., enumerated June 22, 1900; Susan Mashburn-Thompson marriage license, 1887, Montgomery Co., N.C.; 1910 census, Mineral Spring Township, Moore County, N.C., enumerated April 18-19, 1910.

[239] Oppie's birth Jan. 1, 1901 in Oppie Maness Chambers' death certificate, North Carolina, Vital Records Branch, 1986, viewed via Family Search Feb. 21, 2021; and her tombstone, database, *Find a Grave* (http://www.findagrave.com/cgi-bin/fg.cgi?page=gr&GRid=38689952&ref=acom), viewed Jan. 18, 2016. Oppie's birth June 1, 1904 in U.S., Social Security Death Index, 1935-2014, via Ancestry.com; supported by 1930 census (age

26), Flat River township, Person County, enumerated April 5, 1930.

[240] Thurman Maness interview, 2008; Garner, *Tales*, 98-103.

[241] 1860 census, Prosperity [Moore County], N.C., enumerated Aug. 8, 1860; 1860 census, Gold Region, Moore County, N.C., enumerated Aug. 31, 1860; 1850 census, Moore County, N.C., enumerated Nov. 8, 1850, lists a possible family with all six children and mother Mary under the surname Campbell. "Sween" Campbell is 10 years old, which doesn't fit any of Thomas Swain Maness' other records. The other children do fit expected age brackets. George M. Hunsucker lives three houses down the list.

[242] 1870 census, Curriesville, Bensalem Township, Moore County, N.C., enumerated July 16, 1870, 56 (Lundy); enumerated July 18, 1870, 59 (Leanda); 1870 census, Carters Mills, Bensalem Township, Moore County, N.C., enumerated July 25, 1870, 71 (Mary).

[243] George B. Everton Jr. And Louise Mathews Everton, *The Handy Book for Genealogists, United States of America*, Eighth Edition (Logan, Utah: The Everton Publishers, Inc., 1991), 185; Courthouse flood from an undocumented call to the courthouse, ca. 2018 or 2019.

[244] 1880 census, Bensalem Township, Moore County, N.C., enumerated June 1880; 1900 census, Bensalem Township, Moore County, N.C., enumerated June 9-11, 1900; Maness-McCaskill marriage license, Montgomery County, N.C., Dec. 18, 1892.

[245] Maness-McCaskill marriage license; 1900 census, Moore County; 1910 census, South Carthage, Bensalem Township, Moore County, N.C., enumerated April 15, 1910; 1920 census, Ellerbe, Mineral Springs Township, Richmond County, N.C., enumerated March 24, 1920; 1930 census, Asheboro, Randolph County, N.C., enumerated April 10, 1930; Hugh Maness' obituary, *The Courier Tribune* (Asheboro, N.C.), January 13, 1939, 1, Randolph Room, Randolph County Public Library; Mary Jane McCaskill Maness'

obituary, *The Courier Tribune*, February 19, 1939, 1, Randolph Room, Randolph County Public Library.

246 Alexander Maness' tombstone, database, *Find a Grave* (https://www.findagrave.com/memorial/36333305/alexander-maness), viewed June 9, 2022; Lacy Garner, interview by the author, July 24, 2010: My notes say a family in Carthage took in Alexander. He served, and died from injuries after the war. Photo taken by the author at Carthage United Methodist Church cemetery, March 2024.

247 Garner, *Tales*, 188.

248 1880 census, Bensalem township, Moore County, N.C., enumerated June 28, 1880, 211.

249 Maness-McCaskill marriage license, census records, and Maness obituaries.

250 Garner, *Tales*, 188; Arabella Wallace's death certificate, North Carolina, U.S. death certificates, Moore County, 1928, via Ancestry.com; Moore County, N.C., 1928; negative search in N.C. Civil War pension records by the author, via Fold3.

251 Jonas S. Maness' military records; *Moore County Heritage*, 212; Manarin, *NC Troops*, Vol. VII, Infantry, 568; Dorcas Rebecca "Beth" Maness, interview by the author, April 8, 2023.

252 Beth Maness, *Moore County Heritage*, 212; reproduced courtesy of Dorcas Rebecca "Beth" Maness.

253 Bradley Brady's military records; John McGilvary's letter, quoted in Garner, Company H; Manarin, *NC Troops*, Vol. VII, Infantry, 562.

254 1870 census, Prosperity, Ritters Township, Moore County, N.C., enumerated Aug. 11, 1870, 22.

255 Ibid.; 1880 census, Ritters Township, Moore County, N.C., enumerated June 26, 1880, 30.

256 Underwood, 408-409.

[257] "Anniversary of Gettysburg, Forty Years After the Battle," *Charlotte Daily Observer*, Saturday Morning, July 4, 1903 (Charlotte), viewed July 21, 2019, via http://www.26nc.org/Articles/Charlotte%20Daily%20Observerarticleedited.pdf. The story is taken from the 1903 article, however, battlefield guide Eric Lindblade debunks the myth of McConnell shooting Lane in videos at https://www.gettysburgdaily.com/26th-north-carolina-part-5-lbg-eric-lindblade/ (viewed May 28, 2024).

[258] Civil War Veteran John Randolph Lane, photograph by Cyrus P. Wharton, ca. 1890-1910; Liljenquist Family Collection of Civil War Photographs, Library of Congress Prints and Photographs Division, http://hdl.loc.gov/loc.pnp/ppmsca.53104.

[259] 1900 census, Chapel Hill, Chapel Hill Township, Orange County, N.C., enumerated June 5, 1900, 174, sheet 5.

[260] Ibid.

[261] Mary Craton Maness' death certificate, Orange County, N.C., 1915.

[262] 1900 census, Chapel Hill; 1910 census, Chapel Hill Township, Orange County, N.C., enumerated April 23, 1910, sheet 6B.

[263] 1900 census, Chapel Hill; 1910 census, Chapel Hill; William Maner-Pendergrass marriage license, Orange County, N.C., January 5, 1897; death records for single children and negative searches for others.

[264] Gail Gordon, correspondence with the author, 2017-2018; Linda Gail Gordon, "'Taylor' Family Record as of Late 1700's," manuscript, 2017.

[265] Robert and Lula Maynor, undated digital image; Gail Gordon, 2016.

[266] Lula Maynor, undated digital image; Gail Gordon, 2017.

[267] Bob Maynor Sr.'s obituary, undated clipping, digital image; privately held by Gail Gordon, 2017.

268 Ibid.; Robert Maynor's death certificate, North Carolina, Death Certificates, 1909-1975; Lula Maynor's death certificate, North Carolina, U.S., Death Certificates, 1909-1976; Lula Maynor's obituary, undated clipping, Gail Gordon, 2017; Bob and Lula Maynor tombstone, North Chapel Hill Baptist Church cemetery, visited by the author June 16, 2018.

269 Multiple sources, including censuses and cemeteries. For more details, join the community at elizabethasaunders.com.

270 Postcard of the O. Henry Hotel, Greensboro, N.C. (Milwaukee, E. C. Kropp Co.), ca. 1920; privately held by Elizabeth A. Saunders.

271 Sarah Pandora Wall Maness and family, four generations, ca. 1896; Maness Family Collection.

272 Sarah Pandora Wall Maness and family, five generations, ca. 1918; Maness Family Collection.

273 Frank Wiley Maness with some of his children and grandchildren, ca. late 1940s; Maness Family Collection.

274 McAdoo house letter, Maness Family Collection; Maness family oral history; 1880 Census, Sumner Township, Guilford County, enumerated June 8, 1880; Sarah Pandora Maness' death certificate, North Carolina, Death Certificates, 1909-1975, 1930.

275 Frank Vance and Daisy Routh Maness with children, ca. 1935; Maness Family Collection.

276 Sarah P. Wall, Martha Chappell, and Mary Jane Chappell Waldon Priest tombstones, Centre Friends Meeting cemetery, Guilford County, N.C.; William Addison Waldon and Jackson Priest tombstones, Fairfield United Methodist Church cemetery, Guilford County, N.C.; Walton-Priest marriage license, Guilford County, N.C., Feb. 14, 1912; 1900 census, New Market Township, Randolph County, N.C., enumerated July 10, 1900.

277 Pandora's obituary, "Mrs. Sarah Maness Dies At Son's Home," *High Point* (N.C.) *Enterprise,* July 31, 1930, microfilm at High Point Public Library; Sarah P. Maness' death certificate, Randolph County, N.C., 1930.

278 Elizabeth A. Saunders, *Archdale Friends Meeting: Genealogical Extracts from the Monthly Meeting Minutes: 1924-1949* (Baltimore: Gateway Press, 2005); Author's family records and oral history; Maness-English marriage register, N.C. Marriage Records 1741-2011; 1910 census, Trinity Township, Randolph County, enumerated May 10, 1910.

279 Multiple sources, including censuses, obituary clippings, and Frank Wiley Maness' Bible, Maness Family Collection. For more details, join the community at elizabethasaunders.com.

280 1880 census, Pembroke, Giles County, Va., enumerated June 21, 1880; 1900 census, Newport Magisterial District, Giles County, Va., enumerated June 25, 1900; Nancy Maness' death certificate, Pulaski County, Va., 1920.

281 Manes-Sifford marriage index, Virginia Select Marriages 1785-1940, Feb. 5, 1896; 1910 census, Dublin District, Pulaski County, Va., enumerated April 28, 1910; 1920 census, Dublin District, Pulaski County, Va., enumerated Jan. 8, 1920; Manes-Swabey marriage, West Virginia, Marriages Index, 1785-1971, 1910; 1920 census, Columbus, Ward 15, Franklin County, Ohio, enumerated Jan. 4-5, 1920; "Mrs. Agnes Manes et als vs. C. P. Sifford et als," Chancery files, 1924-1932, Circuit Court of Pulaski County, Va; Thomas Manes' obituary, *The Daily Notes* (Canonsburg, Pa.), April 17, 1924, 1.

282 Photograph, Christmas in Pulaski, 1918, courtesy of the Raymond F. Ratclliffe Memorial Transportation Museum, Pulaski, Va.

283 Nancy Maness' death certificate, Pulaski County, Va., 1920; negative search at Brown Cemetery, near Radford, Pulaski County, Va., by the author in 2016; Fannie Sifford's death certificate, Pulaski County, Va., 1921.

284 Fannie Sifford's death certificate.

285 Thomas Manes' obituary; Manes vs. Sifford in Chancery files.

286 1930 census, St. Paul, Wise County, Va., enumerated April 12, 1930; 1940 census, St. Paul, Wise County, Va., enumerated April

18, 1940; 1940 census, Dublin, Pulaski County, Va., enumerated May 6, 1940.

287 Agnes Swabey Maness' obituary, *The Daily Notes*, Jan. 7, 1952.

288 Multiple sources, including death certificates and Virginia county chancery records. For more details, join the community at elizabethasaunders.com.

289 Martin "Marty" A. Maners Jr., interview by the author, April 24, 2021; 1900 census, Lanesboro Township, Anson County, N.C., enumerated June 7, 1900.

290 Maness-Atkinson Marriage Register, North Carolina, Marriage Records, 1741-2011, Anson County, p. 12; 1920 census, Gastonia, Gaston County, N.C., enumerated Jan. 16, 1920; Louisa Kelly's death certificate, Gaston County, N.C., 1930; Marty Maners interview, 2021.

291 Marty Maners interview, 2021; 1940 census, Guilford County, N.C., enumerated April 22, 1940; Herman Fantom Maners' death certificate, North Carolina, U.S., Death Certificates, 1909-1976, Guilford County, N.C., 1967.

292 Marty Maners interview, 2021; Herman Fantom Maners' death certificate; Herman Fantom Maners Sr.'s obituary, *High Point Enterprise*, June 3, 1967, 12.

293 Marty Maners interview, 2021; 1920 census, Gastonia, Gaston County, N.C., enumerated Jan. 13, 1920; 1930 census, Gastonia, Gaston County, N.C., enumerated April 5, 1930; 1940 census, Gastonia, Gaston County, N.C., enumerated April 10, 1940.

294 Maness-Carter marriage license, Gaston County, N.C., July 29, 1912; 1920 census, Gastonia; 1930 census, Gastonia; William Maners' obituary, *The Gastonia* (N.C.) *Gazette*, May 4, 1972, 1.

295 Multiple sources, including death certificates and obituaries from *The Charlotte News* and *The Charlotte Observer*. For more details, join the community at elizabethasaunders.com.

296 Frank Maners' death certificate, Mecklenburg County, N.C., 1958; Frank M. Maners' obituary, *The Charlotte Observer*, Jan. 3, 1997,

67 (5Y); 1940 census, Charlotte, Mecklenberg County, N.C., enumerated April 9, 1940; 1942 Charlotte city directory, 497.

[297] Mark Skidmore, interview by the author, April 21, 2022.

[298] Stewart-Keener marriage index, Alabama, U.S., Marriage Indexes, 1814-1935, Etowah County, 10 (178); 1910 census, Gadsden, Etowah County, Ala., enumerated May 6, 1910; Mrs. Willie A. Keener's obituary, *The Gadsden* (Alabama) *Times*, Feb. 16, 1929, digital image, Warsham/Junkins Genealogy Library, Gadsden Public Library.

[299] 1940 census, Greensport, St. Clair County, Ala., enumerated April 3, 1940; Manes-Foreman marriage in Alabama, U.S. Marriage Indexes, 1814-1935, 1906; 1920 census, Gadsden, Etowah County, Ala., enumerated Jan. 12, 1920; 1930 census, East Gadsden, Etowah County, Ala., enumerated April 17, 1930; Mark Skidmore interview, 2022; Walter Foreman's obituary, Jan. 15, 1923, *The Gadsden Times*, 1, and Jan. 16, 1923, 1.

[300] Willie Stewart's death in Alabama, U.S., Deaths and Burials Index, 1881-1974, FHL film 1908463; Mrs. Willie A. Keener's obituary, *The Gadsden Times*, undated clipping, digital image, Warsham/Junkins Genealogy Library, Gadsden Public Library.

[301] Willie Stewart Manes Keener and John Keener, undated digital image; Elaine Watts, 2021; identified by Mark Skidmore.

[302] Cora and Walter Foreman, undated digital image; Elaine Watts, 2021; identified by Mark Skidmore.

[303] Cora Manes Foreman Walker with children, undated digital image; Elaine Watts, 2021.

[304] Manes-Walker marriage in Alabama, U.S., Marriage Indexes, 1814-1935, Etowah County, 1929, 503; Mark Skidmore interview, 2022; 1940 census, St. Clair County, Ala., enumerated April 3, 1940; Cora Foreman Walker's obituary, *The Gadsden Times*, undated clipping, Warsham/Junkins Genealogy Library, Gadsden Public Library; Thad Walker's obituary, *The Gadsden Times*, undated clipping, Warsham/Junkins Genealogy Library, Gadsden

Public Library; 1950 census, The Bryce Hospital, Tuscaloosa, Tuscaloosa County, Ala., enumerated April 13, 1950; Thad Walker's tombstone, database, *Find a Grave* (https://www.findagrave.com/memorial/87290357/cora-elizabeth-foreman_walker), accessed May 6, 2022.

[305] Cora Manes Foreman Walker's obituary, *The Gadsden Times*, undated clipping, digital image, Warsham/Junkins Genealogy Library, Gadsden Public Library; Cora Manes Foreman Walker's tombstone, database, *Find a Grave* (https://www.findagrave.com/memorial/87290357/cora-elizabeth-foreman_walker), accessed May 6, 2022; Mark Skidmore interview, 2022.

[306] Multiple sources, including censuses and obituaries from *The Gadsden Times* and Legacy.com. For more details, join the community at elizabethasaunders.com.

[307] 1910 census, Mineral Spring township, Moore County, N.C., enumerated April 18-19, 1910; Mashburn-Thompson marriage license, March 3, 1887, Montgomery Co., N.C.; 1910 census, Bensalem township, Moore County, N.C., enumerated May 4, 1910.

[308] Fannie M. Mashburn in 1880 census, Carthage township, Moore County, N.C., June 25, 1880; Fannie A. Jones in 1900 census, Bensalem township, Moore County, N.C., enumerated June 28, 1900.

[309] Annie Mashburn Tucker's death certificate, 1964, Montgomery County, N.C.; Annie Mashburn Tucker's obituary, *The High Point Enterprise*, January 29, 1964, 20.

[309b] Multiple sources, including census and obituaries.

[310] Cora Maness Brown's death certificate, 1994, viewed via Family Search Feb. 21, 2021 (birth date Oct. 1, 1901); Oppie Maness Chambers' death certificate, 1986, viewed via Family Search Feb. 21, 2021 (birth date Jan. 1, 1902); Oppie Maness Chambers' tombstone, database, *Find a Grave* (http://www.findagrave.com/cgi-bin/fg.cgi?page=gr&GRid=38689952&ref=acom, 2009), viewed Jan. 18, 2016 (birth date Jan. 1, 1902); Oppie's

birth date June 1, 1904 in U.S., Social Security Death Index, 1935-2014.

[311] Jones-Brady marriage license, Moore County, 1908; 1910 census, Greenwood township, Moore County, N.C., enumerated May 10, 1910; 1920 census, Ritters township, Moore County, N.C., enumerated Feb. 27, 1920.

[312] Sarah Jones' death certificate, North Carolina, Death Certificates, 1909-1975, Wake County, 1964.

[313] Cora Maness Brown's obituary, *The News and Observer* (Raleigh, N.C.), Nov. 2, 1994, unpaginated clipping from microfilm, High Point Public Library.

[314] Oppie Chambers' obituary, *The Herald Sun* (Durham, N.C.), Oct. 14, 1986, 18.

[315] Multiple sources, including censuses, death certificates, and obituaries from *The News and Observer*. For more details, join the community at elizabethasaunders.com.

INDEX

A

Abernathy, Austin 147
Abernathy, Blanche (Maners) 147
Adams, Cornelia Elizabeth (Foreman) 151
Adams, William V. 151
Addison, Walter D. 56, 63, 66, 68
Alabama 94, 151
  Attalla 92, 94
  Etowah County 94
  Gadsden 94, 149
  Tuscaloosa 151
Albertson, Myrtle. See Maners, Myrtle
Albright, H. C. 30
Anderson, Louise (Maners) 147
Andrews, Annie (Maness) 137, 140
Andrews, F. L. 140
Andrews, Gladys Marie 140
Andrews, Henry Clay 140
Andrews, Henry Clay Jr. 140
Andrews, Levedith (Wheat) 140
Andrews, Margaret Sarah 137, 140
Andrews, Pauline (Kearns) 140
Andrews, Ruby (Bundy) 140
Andrews, Thomas Edward 140
Arkansas 6, 73, 110, 115
Army of Northern Virginia 17, 24, 30, 33, 36, 44
Army of the Potomac 17, 24, 48
Arrington, Lucy Yvonne. See Maness, Lucy Yvonne
Atkinson, Louisa. See Maness, Louisa
Atkinson, Samuel Wilbert 145, 147
Atlantic and North Carolina Railroad 10

B

Bailey, John 77, 103
Bailey, Julia 77
Beane, Carl Clifford 127
Beane, Katherine Mae (Maness) 126, 127
Beane, Shirley (Kennedy) 127
Beane, Vivian C. 127
Beane, William Clifford 127
Berry, Addie Lena. See Maners, Addie Lena
Biddle, Rosa Lee. See Foreman, Rosa Lee
Blackwell, Jessie Mary (Maners) 147
Blackwell, William Clinton 147
Blackwood, Clara M. 133
Blackwood, Floy Valentine (Maynor). See Maynor, Floy Valentine
Blackwood, Hollis Clifton 133
Blackwood, Hollis G. 133
Blackwood, Lavear Beatrice 133
Blackwood, Lucy C. 133
Blackwood, Mary L. 133
Blackwood, Mary (Maynor) 133
Blackwood, Oscar F. 133
Blackwood, Polly 133
Blackwood, Theodore 131–133
Bolli, Clementine Hilda. See Maness, Clementine Hilda
Brady, Bethuel 128
Brady, Bradley 2, 3, 42, 48, 49, 107, 128
Brady, Catherine 107
Brady, Sarah 20, 107, 108, 111, 112, 116, 119, 154–156
Branch, L. O. 10, 11, 59
Britt, Patience. See Jones, Patience
Brockenborough (General) 39
Brooks, Annabelle. See Manes, Annabelle

Brown, Cora Etta (Maness) 107, 108, 111, 113, 116, 119, 155, 156
Brown, Elzie 156
Brown, Herbert Mitchell 111, 155, 156
Brown, Lessie. *See* Williams, Lessie
Brown, Lottie. *See* Flewelling, Lottie
Brown, Myrtle. *See* Tress, Myrtle
Bryce Hospital 151
Buie family 126
Buie, John 77
Buie, Margaret 77
Bullard, Joe 95
Bundy, Blanche 140
Bundy, Frank 140
Bundy, Fred 140
Bundy, Herman 140
Bundy, James 140
Bundy, James Mordecai 140
Bundy, Kenneth Ray 140
Bundy, Mary L. 140
Bundy, Nealie M. (Maness) 140
Bundy, Roland W. 140
Bundy, Ruby 140
Bundy, Verly M. 140
Burgwyn, Henry K. Jr. 2, 3, 10, 11, 15, 16, 26, 29, 30, 39–41, 47, 57
Burgwyn, William H. S. 57, 75
Burnett, Emma Bertie (Morgan) 154
Burnett, William 154
Burney, Dora (Franklin) Pitt 140
Burney, Lee 140

C

Camp Crabtree 2, 3
Camp Wilkes 9
Carmichael, A. B. 16
Chambers, Francis 156
Chambers, Gertrude 156
Chambers, Herman 156
Chambers, James Edgar 156
Chambers, Lucille 156
Chambers, Minnie Marie 156
Chambers, Oppie (Maness) 108, 119, 155, 156
Chappell, Gilbert 13, 81, 82
Chappell, Jonathan 81
Chappell, Martha (Gossett) Wall 14, 81, 82, 136–138
Chappell, Mary Jane 82, 138
Chesapeake Bay 51–53, 55
Company D, 49th Regiment, N.C. Troops 32, 60
Company G, 46th Regiment, N.C. Troops 75
Company H, 26th N.C. Troops viii, 2, 4, 9, 16, 23, 30, 40, 43, 44, 175–178, 189
Company I, 2nd N.C. Cavalry 10
Company I, 49th Regiment, N.C. Troops 59
conscription 29, 31, 75
Cox, Robert 43
Craton, Mary 77, 131, 133
Crayton, Mary. *See* Craton, Mary
Crouse, Rebecca (Maness). *See* Poteat, Rebecca
Crouse, Richard Lane 140
Cureton, Thomas J. 16

D

Dagsher, John 144
Dagsher, Nannie Edith (Manes) 144
Dale, Florence (Maness) 137–140
Dale, James H. 139, 140
Dandridge, T. W. 62
Davidson, Carol Ann (Wesley) 140
Davidson, Tim 140
Davis, Treva (Franklin) 140
Davis, Walter 140
Day, William A. 59, 61
Delaware 68

INDEX

Delk, Carolyn Christine (Maness) 127
Delk, Charles Ray Sr. 127
desertion, deserters 29, 43, 49, 56, 75, 128
Dibrell, Richard 67
District of Columbia 57
  Old Capitol Prison 36
  Washington 13, 36, 48, 57, 68
DNA genealogy 21, 89, 98, 100, 101, 110, 116, 155
  autosomal DNA 115–117, 128
  Family Tree DNA 99, 116
  mitochondrial DNA 110, 116
  Y-DNA 99, 100, 110, 157
Dowd, Clement 16
Dowd, John 77
Dowd, Mary 77
Dugan, Lucy E.. *See* Maners, Lucy E.
dysentery 44, 65

E

Eggleston, George C. 60, 61
Ellis, Governor of North Carolina 3
Ellis, Peter 26
England 80
English, Emma. *See* Maness, Emma (English)
English family 73

F

Fairfield United Methodist Church 138
Flewelling, Lottie (Brown) 155
Foreman, Charles E. 151
Foreman, Cora (Manes). *See* Manes, Cora Elizabeth
Foreman, Cornelia Elizabeth 151
Foreman, Esther Mae 151
Foreman, Eugene 151
Foreman, Gladys. *See* Skidmore, Gladys
Foreman, Myrtle 151
Foreman, Rosa Lee (Biddle) 151
Foreman, Ruby 151
Foreman, Samuel Fred 151
Foreman, Samuel Walter 149–151
Foreman, Willie Mae (Freeman) 151
Fort Hatteras 3
Fort Macon 3
Fort Thompson 10
Forty-Ninth Regiment, North Carolina Troops 32, 59–62, 167, 179
Franklin, Dennis Levi 140
Franklin, Dora Mae 140
Franklin, Earma 140
Franklin, Leatrice 140
Franklin, Lena 140
Franklin, Pearl (Maness). *See* Maness, Pearl
Franklin, Peggy 140
Franklin, Samuel Levi 137, 140
Franklin, Treva 140
Freeman, Willie Mae. *See* Foreman, Willie Mae
Frost, Katherine. *See* Lipscomb, Katherine

G

Gaither, W. W. 48
Gall, Iva May (Manes) 144
Gall, Michael 144
gangrene 66
Garner, Lacy A. Jr. 21, 80, 89, 95–100, 101, 159, 189
Gass, Fannie Mozelle (Jones) 154
Gass, Wallace Walker 154
Gaster, Gertrude (Chambers) Painter 156
Gaster, Otis 156
Georgia 67, 89, 145
  Savannah 67
Gordon, Gail 131–132
Gossett family 81

Gossett, Martha. *See* Chappell, Martha
Graham, William A. 15, 16, 33, 34, 36
Gramling, Wilbur 67
Grant, Eula Mae (Robinson) 127
Grant (General) 48, 49, 55, 60
Grant, James Lacy Sr. 127
Grant, Loyd Odell Sr. 127
Grant, Malone L. 127
Grant, Mary L. (Maness) 126, 127
Grant, Nellie (Quick) 127
Grant, Rachel 127
Grant, Ruby Mae 127
Grant, Ruth 127
Grant, Thelma 127

H

Haley, Michael J. 65
Hancock, Dovie Alice. *See* McIntosh, Dovie Alice
Henderson, Suzanne K. 116
Hensen, Mary 73
Hepler, Blanche (Bundy) 140
Hepler, J. H. 140
Heth (General) 39
Hicks, Anita Louise 127
Hicks, Anne Marie (Snider) 127
Hicks, Barbara Lorene (Jarrell) 127
Hicks, Claude Lee Jr. 127
Hicks, Claude Lee Sr. 127
Hicks, Delette 127
Hicks, Diane 127
Hicks, Eugene Dowd 127
Hicks, Glenn 127
Hicks, Hal Alexander 127
Hicks, Ida Lee (Maness) 126, 127
Hicks, James Winfred 127
Hicks, Mary Jewel 127
Hicks, Nellie (Kivett) 127
Hicks, Nellie Ruth 127
Hicks, Phyllis Ruth (Womer) 127
Hightower, Debbie S. 80
Hightower, Edwin K. III 80

Hill, Annie (Maynor) 133
Hill, Bob 133
Hill, Joan. *See* Maness, Joan
Hilton, Barbara E.. *See* Sifford, Barbara E.
hospitals, Civil War
  Hammond General Hospital, Md. 55, 57
  Hospital in Elmira prison camp, N.Y. 64, 68
  Hospital in Petersburg, Va. 44
  Hospital in Richmond, Va. 91
  Hospital near Morehead City, N.C. 4
  Poplar Lawn Park, Va. 44
  Union hospital in Pennsylvania 48
  Wayside Hospital, Va. 44
  Winder Hospital, Va. 44
House, Margaret (Andrews) 137, 140
House, Wilford James 140
Huger (General) 24
Hundley, Fannie. *See* Maynor, Fannie
Hunsucker, George 104, 157
Hutt, Charles Warren 55, 56

I

Ireland 80
Iron Brigade. *See* Nineteenth Regiment, Indiana or Twenty-fourth Regiment, Michigan

J

Jackson, Morgan 159
Jarrell, Barbara Lorene. *See* Hicks, Barbara Lorene
Johnson, Christopher Lane 159
Johnson, Diane (Hicks) 127
Johnson family 94
Johnson, Jimmy 127
Jones, Charlie Garland 155, 156

INDEX

Jones, Christopher 104, 153, 154
Jones, Elizabeth 156
Jones, Fannie 153. *See* Mashburn, Fannie
Jones, Fannie Mozelle 154
Jones, Faraby Jane. *See* Mashburn, Faraby Jane
Jones, Frank 154–156
Jones, James C. 154
Jones, John T. 30, 39, 41, 47, 48
Jones, Lilly 155, 156
Jones, Lizzie 155
Jones, Lloyd 155, 156
Jones, Lovedy Jane 154
Jones, Martin 103, 154
Jones, Patience (Britt) 154
Jones, Penelope (Mashburn) 103, 154
Jones, Peter 43
Jones, Sarah (Brady) Maness. *See* Brady, Sarah
Jones, Sarah (Chris' daughter) 154

K

Kearns, Edwin S. 140
Kearns, Lena (Franklin) 140
Kearns, Pauline. *See* Andrews, Pauline
Keener, Clara Mae 149, 151
Keener, John Thomas 149, 150, 151
Keener, Willie. *See* Stewart, Willie
Keener, Willie Sue 149, 151
Kelly, Louisa 158. *See* Maness, Louisa
Kelly, Louiza (mother) 91, 94
Kelly, Martin 91
Kennedy, Shirley. *See* Beane, Shirley
Kentucky 115
Kerns, Lucille (Chambers) 156
Kerns, Roy Jackson 156
Kilpatrick, Judson 91
King, John R. 68
Kirkland (General) 45, 48, 49

Kivett, Nellie. *See* Hicks, Nellie

L

Lane, John R. 2, 4, 26, 30, 40, 41, 44, 47, 48, 128, 129
Lawder, Doris Sue (Lipscomb) 151
Lawder, John 151
Lawson, Esther Mae (Foreman) 151
Lawson, Woodson 151
Lee, Earma (Franklin) Stinson 140
Lee, Robert E. 17, 24, 30, 33, 34, 36, 39, 48, 49, 59, 68
Lee, Rosie Etta. *See* Maners, Rosie Etta
Lee, W. H. F. 33, 35
Lefler, Bertha Lee. *See* Maness, Bertha Lee
Leon, Lewis 67
Lewis, B. G. 43
Lewis, Etta Belle 127
lice 66, 68
Lincoln, Abraham 3, 55
Lipscomb, A. Linder 151
Lipscomb, Ann 151
Lipscomb, Benjamin F. 151
Lipscomb, Clara Mae (Keener) 149, 151
Lipscomb, Delma Martin 151
Lipscomb, Doris Sue 151
Lipscomb, Douglas Graves 151
Lipscomb, John Thomas 151
Lipscomb, Katherine (Frost) 151
Lipscomb, Willie Sue (Keener) 149, 151
Long, Mazie. *See* Maners, Mazie
Longstreet (General) 48
Lutz, Shirley. *See* Maners, Shirley
Lyons, Jan 151
Lyons, Mary Frances (Walker) 151

M

Magruder (General) 24
Malvern Hill. *See* Virginia

Maners, Addie Lena (Berry) 145, 146, 147
Maners, Annie Marie (Smith) 147
Maners, Betty Lois (Mullis) 147
Maners, Blanche 147
Maners, Emory 147
Maners, Fannie (Platt) 147
Maners, Frank 147
Maners, Frank Mason 147
Maners, Georgia (Reynolds) 147
Maners, Gracie 147
Maners, Hampton. See Maners, Herman Fantom
Maners, Harvey William Sr. (Frank's son) 147
Maners, Harvey William (William Harvey's son) 147
Maners, Herman Fantom 94, 145–147
Maners, Herman Fantom Jr. 147
Maners, Jesse Waldo 147
Maners, Jessie Mary 147
Maners, Lamar 147
Maners, Leona (Sigmon) 147
Maners, Louise 147
Maners, Lucy E. (Dugan) 147
Maners, Martin Adolphus 147
Maners, Martin A. Jr. 145
Maners, Mary Magdalene 147
Maners, Mazie (Long) 147
Maners, Myrtle (Albertson) 147
Maners, Olin Donald 147
Maners, Rosie Etta (Lee) 147
Maners, Roy Albert 147
Maners, Ruth (Sloan) 145, 147
Maners, Shirley (Lutz) 147
Maners, Velma Irene (Morgan) 147
Maners, Vera Othella 147
Maners, Vera (Westbrooks) 147
Maners, William Harvey 94, 145, 147
Maners, William Thomas 147
Manes, Agnes (Swabey) 141, 143, 144
Manes, Annabelle (Brooks) 144

Manes, Clara Agnes 144
Manes, Cora Elizabeth 149–151
Manes, Edward James 144
Manes, Herman Fantom. See Maners
Manes, Iva May 144
Manes, John Harvey 144
Manes, Nannie Edith 144
Maness, Abednego 20, 73, 99
Maness, Alexander L. 2, 9, 10, 15, 20, 31, 33–37, 48, 49, 57, 58, 68, 75–77, 125, 126, 161, 162, 172, 176, 178, 179, 182, 189
Maness, Becky. See Poteat, Rebecca
Maness, Bertha Lee (Lefler) 127
Maness, Bessie. See Saunders, Bessie
Maness, Carolyn Christine 127
Maness, Clementine Hilda (Bolli) 127
Maness, Clyde Lenox 127
Maness, Cora Elizabeth 94
Maness, Cora Etta. See Brown, Cora
Maness, Daisy (Routh) 5, 6, 14, 96, 137–140
Maness, Daniel Alexander Jr. 127
Maness, Daniel Alexander Sr. 126, 127
Maness, David 140
Maness, Emma (English) 6, 7, 137, 138, 140
Maness, Etta Belle (Lewis) 127
Maness, Fannie Betty. See Sifford, Fannie
Maness, Frank (Anson Co.). See Maners, Frank
Maness, Frank Oscar 5–7, 14, 19, 20, 21, 73, 79, 80, 95, 96, 98–100, 109, 116, 117, 138–140, 184
Maness, Frank Vance vii, 5, 6, 7, 14, 73, 96, 116, 137–140

Index

Maness, Frank Wiley 6, 13, 73, 82, 83, 96, 97, 101, 116, 135–140
Maness, Henry 20, 21, 95, 100, 115, 125, 126, 157
Maness, Hugh Alexander 77, 126, 127
Maness, Ida Lee. *See* Hicks, Ida Lee
Maness, Ira Lane 23, 29, 31, 43, 77, 119, 120, 126
Maness, Isaac Jr. 29, 43, 75
Maness, James Calvi 126
Maness, James Calvin "Callie" 127
Maness, James Harold Sr. 127
Maness, James Robert. *See* Maynor, James Robert
Maness, Joan (Hill) 127
Maness, John Madison 137, 139, 140
Maness, John William 139, 140
Maness, Jonas Sedberry 2, 3, 42, 48, 49, 128
Maness, Joyce (Yow) 140
Maness, Katherine Mae. *See* Beane, Katherine Mae
Maness, Leanda Cain 20, 77, 125
Maness, Lewis Ray 127
Maness, Louisa (Kelly) 91, 94, 145–147
Maness, Lucy Yvonne (Arrington) 127
Maness, Lundy Jane 20, 77, 125, 126
Maness, Mardecia (Hopkins) 127
Maness, Martha (daughter) 78, 131, 133
Maness, Martha J. (Mashburn). *See* Mashburn, Martha J.
Maness, Mary (author's great-aunt). *See* Payseur, Mary
Maness, Mary (Craton). *See* Craton, Mary
Maness, Mary C. (sister) 20, 31, 77, 103, 125

Maness, Mary Jane (McCaskill). *See* McCaskill, Mary Jane
Maness, Mary L.. *See* Grant, Mary L.
Maness, Mary "Polly" 14, 21, 73, 82, 86, 100, 104, 110, 157
Maness, Meshach 20, 73, 99
Maness, Nancy (Pool) 86, 94, 141, 143, 158
Maness, Nealie M. 140
Maness, Oppie. *See* Chambers, Oppie
Maness, Oscar 139
Maness, Pearl 136, 137, 140
Maness, Pearl Estelle. *See* Shaw, Pearl Estelle
Maness, Penny (Presnell) 140
Maness, Philip Martin 139, 140
Maness, Reuben I 75, 76, 77, 119
Maness, Reuben II 98, 119, 120, 121
Maness, Sarah Annie 137, 140
Maness, Sarah (Brady). *See* Brady, Sarah
Maness, Sarah Pandora (Wall) 6, 13, 14, 20, 81, 82, 115, 135–138, 140, 141, 157, 158
Maness, Shadrach 2, 20, 31, 32, 59, 61, 62, 76, 77, 91, 98, 125–127
Maness, Shadrach I (triplet) 20, 73, 99
Maness, Sondra (Stone) 140
Maness, Thomas Lee 140
Maness, Thomas P. 75, 76, 96, 97, 119
Maness, Thomas S. 6
  age 1, 14, 21, 68, 77, 82, 86, 103, 104, 157, 158, 161
  avoiding battles 43, 44
  battles 10, 15, 25, 48, 49
  enlistment 1, 17, 67
  in prison 43, 55, 56, 58, 63, 64, 66, 68, 69
  marriage 77, 81, 86, 94, 104, 107

parents 14, 20, 21, 73, 82, 86, 95, 100, 104, 110, 115, 125, 157, 161
potential photos 96
Swain Maness stories 20, 21, 88, 89, 98–100, 101, 110, 116, 119, 120
work 81, 82, 85, 86, 88, 89, 94, 101
Maness, Thurman D. vii, viii, 19, 20, 21, 73, 76, 80, 87–89, 95, 97–100, 111, 115, 116, 119, 126, 157–159, 162, 164, 169, 175, 178, 182, 185, 188
Maness, Tommy P. 96, 97, 119
Maness, Treva (Presnell) 137, 140
Maness, Verdia 19, 80, 87
Maness, William Clay 126, 127
Maness, William Harvey. *See* Maners, William Harvey
Maness, William I 20
Maness, William II "Billy" 20
Maness, William Nuton. *See* Maynor, William Nuton
Maness, Willie (Stewart). *See* Stewart, Willie
Manes, Thomas Cleveland 94, 141, 143, 144
Manes, Thomas William 144
Martin, Claude 127
Martin, Ruth (Grant) 127
Martin, William P. 1, 16
Maryland 13, 79, 116
  Baltimore 57
  Patuxent River Naval Air Station 13
  Point Lookout 51–53, 55. *See also* Prison camps
  Southern Maryland 5, 51, 71
Mashburn, Annie. *See* Morgan, Annie
Mashburn, Fannie 153, 154
Mashburn, Faraby Jane 103, 104, 154

Mashburn, Martha J. 104–108, 153–155, 157, 158
Mashburn, Penelope 154. *See* Jones, Penelope
Mashburn, Susan. *See* Thompson, Susan
Maynor, Annie 133
Maynor, Barbara Carolyn 133
Maynor, Blanche 133
Maynor, Blanche Mae (Stout) 133
Maynor, Charles 133
Maynor, Clyde J. 133
Maynor, Elsie Webb 133
Maynor, Emma Louvenia 133
Maynor, Fannie (Hundley) 133
Maynor, Fletcher Hugh 133
Maynor, Floy Valentine 131, 133
Maynor, Henry Horace 133
Maynor, James Robert 77, 131, 132, 133
Maynor, Lavear Beatrice (Blackwood). *See* Blackwood, Lavear Beatrice
Maynor, Lula (Mincey). *See* Mincey, Lula
Maynor, Margaret Elizabeth 133
Maynor, Mary 133
Maynor, Mollie (Pendergrast) 131, 133
Maynor, Patsy Larue 133
Maynor, Reba Jean 133
Maynor, Robert Jr. 133
Maynor, Ronald 133
Maynor, Rose Annell 133
Maynor, Samuel 133
Maynor, Thomas 133
Maynor, William Nuton 77, 131, 132, 133
McAdoo House 135
McCaskill, Don 73, 111, 159
McCaskill, Mary Jane 126, 127
McClellan, George B. 17
McConnell, Charles H. 129
McCreery (Captain) 40

Index

McIntosh, Dovie Alice (Hancock) 154
McIntosh, Neill 103, 154
measles 4, 32
Michigan 129
Mickey (Captain) 47
Mincey, Lula 131, 132, 133
Missouri 151
Mitropulos, May E. (Sifford) 144
Moore County Boys 2, 37
Moore County Independents. *See* Company H
Moore County, N.C. 1, 3, 29, 31, 73, 78, 91, 94, 96, 97, 103, 108, 112, 115, 119, 125–127, 157
  Bensalem Township 77, 104, 153
  Carter's Mills 77, 78, 103
  Carthage 1, 9, 32, 75, 78, 80, 89, 96, 183, 185, 187–189, 195
  Courthouse 88, 125
  Curriesville 77–78
  Gold Region 31, 77–78
  Highfalls 78, 107
  Mineral Spring 78, 153
  Mount Carmel 104, 107
  Pinehurst 80
  Pleasant Hill Methodist Church 76, 77, 119, 126
  Prosperity 31, 77, 78, 128
  Ritters Township 31, 78, 107
  Robbins 78, 119
  Sheffields Township 31, 78
  Southern Pines 80, 87, 98
Morgan, Annie (Mashburn) 153, 154
Morgan, Emma Bertie 154
Morgan, Essie (Thompson) 154
Morgan, George Withrow Sr. 154
Morgan, Hal Ledbetter 154
Morgan, James B. 154
Morgan, James Terry 154
Morgan, Mary E. 154
Morgan, Mary (Ritter) 154
Morgan, Mary T. 154
Morgan, Thomas Haywood 154
Morgan, Velma Irene. *See* Maners, Velma Irene
Morgan, William 154
Morgan, Zora Lee 154
Morris, Billy Tom 147
Morris, Jessie Mary (Maners) 147
Morrow, Henry 40
Mullis, Betty Lois. *See* Maners, Betty Lois

N

National Archives 13
Newton, Mary Magdalene (Maners) 147
Newton, Rodney V. Sr. 147
New York 56
  Chemung River 63, 68
  Elmira 63, 66, 68
  Foster's Pond 64, 66
Nineteenth Regiment. *See* Second Regiment North Carolina Cavalry
Nineteenth Regiment, Indiana Troops 40
North Carolina 37, 59, 68, 73, 85, 86, 145, 155
  Anson County 91, 94, 145
  Archdale 138
  Asheboro 111, 113, 126, 139
  Bogue Banks 3, 4, 9, 171
  Bogue Sound 4
  Bryce's Creek 10, 11, 15
  Burlington 2
  Cape Fear 17
  Centre community 81, 138
  Chapel Hill 131
  Charlotte 147
  Chatham County 72, 77, 129, 131
  Company Shops 2
  Davidson County 139
  Deep River 81
  Eden 128
  Gaston County 145, 147

Gastonia 145
Goldsboro 32, 59, 165, 167, 171, 172, 180
Greensboro 75, 135
Guilford County 6, 81, 126, 138, 145
High Point 145
Johnston County 111
Kenansville 32
Kinston 16, 59
Lanesboro Township 94, 145
Mecklenburg County 147
Moore County. *See* Moore County, N.C.
Morehead City 3, 4
Neuse River 10
New Bern 9, 10, 16, 30, 33, 59, 168
Orange County 131
Otter Creek 10
Outer Banks 9
Person County 156
Pittsboro 72, 73, 77
Raleigh 2, 3, 13, 14, 20, 155, 157
Randolph County 20, 21, 79, 81, 88, 89, 98, 109, 115, 126, 128, 138, 139
Siler City 72, 73
Wadesboro 93–94
Wake County 86
Washington 30
White Store 94
White Store Township 91
Wilmington 17, 32
North Carolina Railroad Company 2
North Carolina State Archives 14

O

O. Henry Hotel 135
Ohio 141
Opie, John 67
Orange United Methodist Church 131

P

Painter, Gertrude (Chambers) 156
Painter, James 156
Payseur, Baxter 140
Payseur, Mary (Maness) 72, 73, 137, 140
Peele, Elizabeth (Jones) 156
Peele, William Victor 156
Pendergrast, Mollie Jane. *See* Maynor, Mollie
Pennsylvania 37, 43, 44, 143
  Canonsburg 141
  Cashtown 37
  Gettysburg 37, 39, 41, 42, 44, 47–49, 52, 55, 59, 128, 129, 163, 164, 167, 171, 175, 177, 189
  McPherson's woods 40
  Philadelphia 57
  Willoughby's Run 40, 43
Pettigrew, James J. 30, 39–41, 44, 45, 47
Pike, Bonnie L. (Walker) 151
Pike, James L. 151
Pitt, Archie Custis 140
Pitt, Dora Mae (Franklin) 140
Platt, Fannie. *See* Maners, Fannie
Pleasant Hill Church. *See* Moore County, N.C.
Pleasanton, Alfred 34
Pool, Charles 86
Pool, Matilda 86
Pool, Moses 86
Pool, Nancy. *See* Maness, Nancy
Porterfield family 141
Poteat, Rebecca (Maness) 101, 139, 140
Poteat, Thomas W. 140
Potomac River 37, 44, 51, 53, 56
Presnell, Penny. *See* Maness, Penny
Presnell, Treva. *See* Maness, Treva
Prison camps, Civil War
  Camp Hoffman. *See* Point Lookout

INDEX

David's Island, N.Y. 48
Elmira, N.Y. 56, 63–66, 68
Fort Delaware, Del. 57, 58, 75
guards 56, 64, 65
Old Capitol Prison, D.C. 36, 48, 57
Point Lookout, Md. 49, 52, 55–58, 63
Washington (Old Capitol) 57

Q

Quakers 52, 73, 80, 81, 138
  Archdale Friends Meeting 138
  Baltimore Friends 81
  Centre Friends Meeting 81, 138
  Centre Friends school 81
  Providence Friends school 81
  Springfield Friends Meeting 138
Quick, Nellie. *See* Grant, Nellie

R

Randolph Rangers. *See* Company G, 46th Regiment
Randolph Room, Randolph County Public Library 111
Ransom, Matt 59, 60
Ransom, Robert 16, 23, 24, 26, 29
Reaves, Harry David Sr. 140
Reaves, Margaret (Andrews) House 137, 140
Reynolds, Georgia. *See* Maners, Georgia
Rich, Joe 127
Rich, Mary Jewel (Hicks) 127
Ritter, Mary. *See* Morgan, Mary
Robbins, L. C. 140
Robbins, Mary L. (Bundy) 140
Robinson, Eula Mae. *See* Grant, Eula Mae
Roulhac, Thomas 60

S

Saunders, Austin O. 140

Saunders, Bessie (Maness) vii, 5, 7, 19–21, 73, 79, 112, 137, 138, 140
Saunders, Elizabeth A. "Beth" 120, 139
Scarborough, Fred 151
Scarborough, Myrtle (Foreman) 151
Scotland 20, 80, 100
scurvy 65
Seaver, Randy 112
Second Regiment, Massachusetts Cavalry 55
Second Regiment North Carolina Cavalry 9, 15, 33, 34, 35, 48
Self, Delette (Hicks) 127
Self, Neil 127
Shady Knoll Gamebird Farm 139
Shaw, Betty Ann 127
Shaw, Howard Carson 127
Shaw, Mark H. 127
Shaw, Max 127
Shaw, Pearl Estelle (Maness) 126, 127
Sheets, Clara Agnes (Manes) 144
Sheets, Clyde Eugene 144
Sherman (General) 91
Shirah, Thelma (Grant) 127
Sifford, Barbara E. (Hilton) 144
Sifford, Charles 141, 143, 144
Sifford, Fannie Betty (Maness) 86, 141, 143, 144
Sifford, Harmon 143
Sifford, Herman Frank 144
Sifford, James Boyce 144
Sifford, Loula R. 144
Sifford, Margie Ann 144
Sifford, May E. 144
Sifford, Nannie 143, 144
Sigmon, Leona. *See* Maners, Leona
Skidmore, Gladys (Foreman) 149, 151
Skidmore, Mark 150
Skidmore, Paul E. 151
Sloan, Ruth. *See* Maners, Ruth

smallpox 55, 65, 67
Smith, Annie Marie. *See* Maners, Annie Marie
Snider, Anne Marie. *See* Hicks, Anne Marie
Snipes, Marvin Roger 147
Snipes, Vera Othella (Maners/Manus) 147
South Carolina 20, 88, 91
Southern Express Railroad 92, 94
Sparks, Emory 147
Sparks, Vincent 147
Stanton, David E. 144
Stanton, Edwin 65
Stanton, Nannie (Sifford) 143, 144
Steen, Ellison Jerry 127
Steen, Ruby Mae (Grant) 127
Steinhof, Anita Louise (Hicks) 127
Steinhof, Eddie 127
Stewart, Willie 94, 149–151, 158
Stinson, Earma (Franklin) 140
Stinson, Gaylord 140
Stone, Sondra A.. *See* Maness, Sondra
Stout, Blanche Mae. *See* Maynor, Blanche Mae
Stuart, J. E. B. 33
Stutts, Dempsey 77
Stutts, Dumps 77
Stutts family 153
Swabey, Agnes. *See* Manes, Agnes

T

Taylor, A. Gustavia 133
Taylor, Alice Laura 133
Taylor, Charlie 133
Taylor, Emma Louvenia (Maynor) 133
Taylor, Hubert G. 133
Taylor, Johnny H. 133
Taylor, Mary 133
Taylor, Ollin Jr. 133
Taylor, Ollin Spencer 133
Taylor, Rena Belle 133
Taylor, Thomas 133
Tennessee 115
Thirty-Third Regiment, North Carolina Troops 10
Thompson, Essie. *See* Morgan, Essie
Thompson, John Jackson 153–154
Thompson, Susan (Mashburn) 103, 153, 154
Thompson, Zora Lee (Morgan) 154
Treadway, James 94
Tress, Myrtle (Brown) 112, 155
Tucker, Annie (Mashburn) Morgan. *See* Morgan, Annie
Tucker, Thomas P. 154
Turner, Edgar G. 127
Turner, Rachel (Grant) 127
Twenty-Fifth Regiment, N.C. Troops 60
Twenty-fourth Regiment, Michigan Troops 40, 129
Twenty-Sixth Regiment, North Carolina Troops viii, 2, 3, 10, 11, 16, 23, 24, 26, 30, 36, 37, 39, 40, 42, 45, 47, 48, 75, 128, 129, 167, 171

U

Underwood, George C. 24, 40
Union (ship) 9

V

Vance, Zebulon B. 3, 4, 10–12, 15, 16, 17, 29
Vass, L. C. 85
Virginia 17, 30, 32, 33, 36, 48, 51, 56, 59, 86, 94, 110, 128, 135, 143, 151
  Appomattox River 36, 60
  Avery's farm 61
  Belspring 141, 143
  Bermuda Hundred 60

INDEX

Bertha Zinc Mine 6, 14, 82, 85, 86
Beverly Ford 34
Blandford Church 62, 75, 76
Brandy Station 34, 35, 176
Bristoe Station 45, 48
Brown's Cemetery 143
Chickahominy 49
Chickahominy River 24
City Point 36, 37, 48, 75
Cold Harbor 49
Culpepper Courthouse 34
Danville 75
Drewry's Bluff 60, 91
Dublin 93–94
Fleetwood Hill 35
Fredericksburg 33, 36
Giles County 86, 141
James River 24, 49, 60
Kelly's Ford 35
Malvern Hill 23, 24, 25, 26, 29, 49, 165, 174
New River 141
Orange County Courthouse 44, 48
Petersburg 23, 43, 44, 59–62, 75, 76, 119, 126, 163, 165, 178, 180
Pulaski 85, 86, 141, 142
Pulaski County 85, 86, 141, 143
Radford 141
Rapidan River 48
Rappahannock River 33, 34
Reams' Station 128
Richmond 17, 23, 26, 29, 30, 36, 44, 49, 60, 61, 68, 75, 91, 187, 188
Ruffin's Run 35
Shenandoah Valley 36
Wilderness 48, 128
Yellow Tavern 128

W

Wakeman, Rosetta (alias Lyons) 3
Walker, Bonnie 151
Walker, Cora (Manes) Foreman. *See* Manes, Cora Elizabeth
Walker, Mary Frances 151
Walker, Thad William 149, 151
Wall, Jimmie 81
Wall, Jonathan Wiley 82
Wall, Martha (Gossett). *See* Chappell, Martha
Wall, Sarah Pandora. *See* Maness, Sarah Pandora
Wallace, Arabella 31, 126, 128, 189
Wallace, Bettie 126
Wallace, Charlotte 126
Wallace, Eli 126
Wallace, Eliza Alice 126
Wallace, James L. 126
Wallace, Jesse Lewis 126
Wallace, Martha 31, 126
Wallace, Nancy 126
Wallace, Quimby 31, 98, 125–127
Wallace, Rufus 126
Wallace, William Wesley 31, 126
Watts, Elaine 150
Weant, Larry 127
Weant, Vivian C. (Beane) 127
Wells, Leatrice (Franklin) 140
Wells, Lester 140
Wesley, Arthur L. Jr. 140
Wesley, Carol Ann 140
Westbrooks, Vera 147
West Virginia 86, 141
Wheat, Levedith. *See* Andrews, Levedith
Wikstrom, Minnie Marie (Chambers) 156
Wikstrom, Walter 156
Wilcox, George 40
Wiley, Norwood 82
Williams, Lessie (Brown) 111–113, 115–117, 155, 156
Williams, Martin 156
Williams, Solomon 34, 35, 36
Wilson, Annon Woods 156

Wilson, Elizabeth (Jones) Peele
   156
Womer, Phyllis Ruth. *See* Hicks,
   Phyllis Ruth

Y

Yow, Joyce. *See* Maness, Joyce

www.ingramcontent.com/pod-product-compliance
Lightning Source LLC
LaVergne TN
LVHW020754250425
809540LV00007B/19